I0181751

A MOTHER'S CRY

BY
ELVA "PRECIOUS LOVE" THOMPSON

Esquire
Publications
"Your Voice In Print!"

Esquire Publications
P. O. Box 352234
Palm Coast, FL 32135-2234

Esquire Publications
P. O. Box 352234
Palm Coast, FL 32135-2234
www.esquirepublications.com
Tel: 1-800-501-7640

"A Mother's Cry"

Copyright © 2001 by Elva "Precious Love" Thompson

Edited by: Michael LiCastri
Cover Art Design by: Designs Unparallel – www.designsunparallel.net

This book is a work of nonfiction. All rights reserved. No part of this book may be reproduced or transmitted in any form or by any means, electronic or mechanical, including photocopying and recording, or by any information storage and retrieval system, without permission in writing from the publisher.

First Edition May 2007
Second Edition October 2009
Third Edition March 2010
Fourth Edition February 2011

Library of Congress Cataloging-in-Publication Data

Library of Congress Control Number: 2010923210

ISBN: 9780982669006

Printed in the United States of America

This book is dedicated to
Amber, Ashley, and *Angel*

With the help of God...we
made it through the storm.

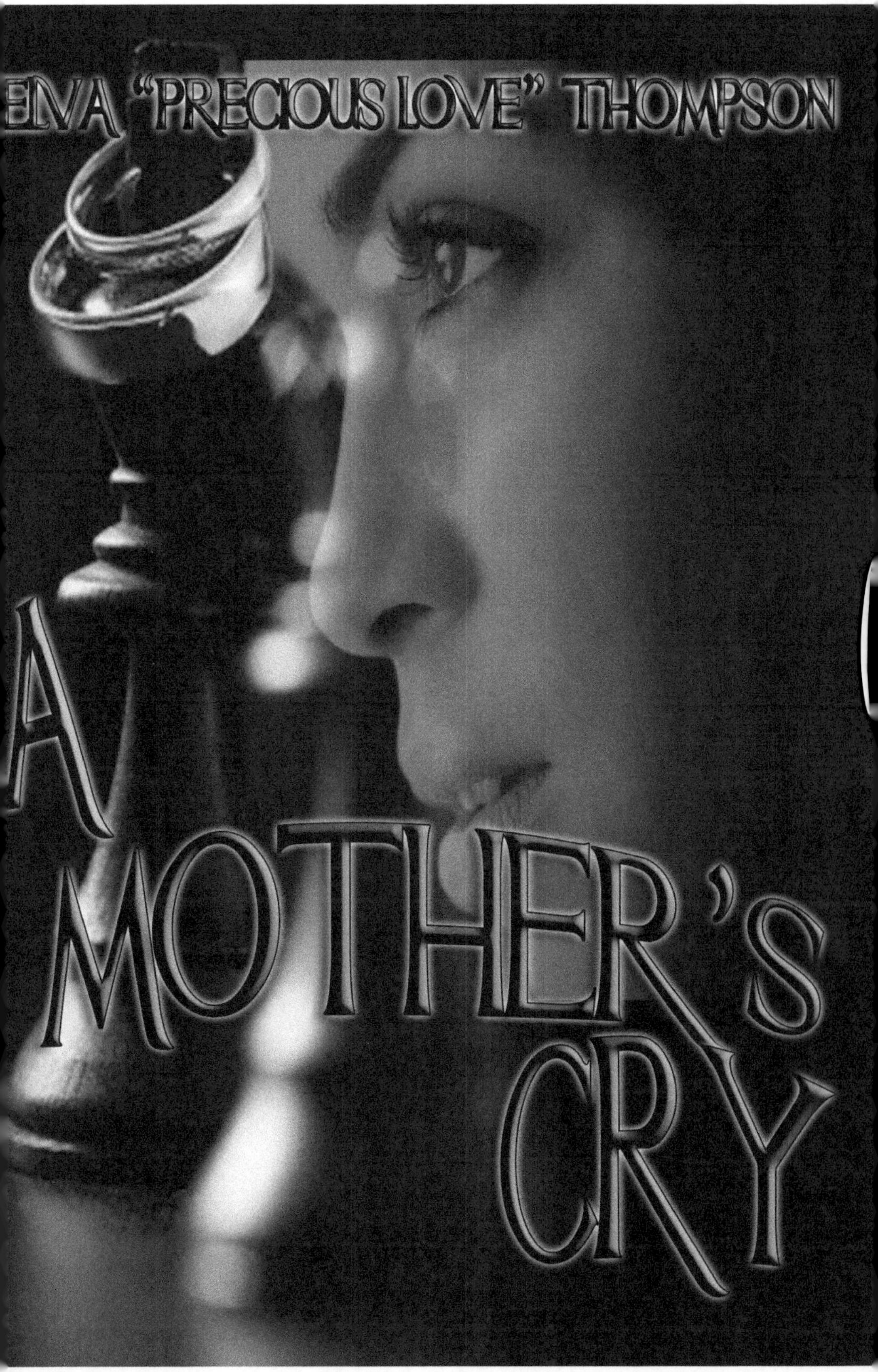
ELVA "PRECIOUS LOVE" THOMPSON
A MOTHER'S CRY

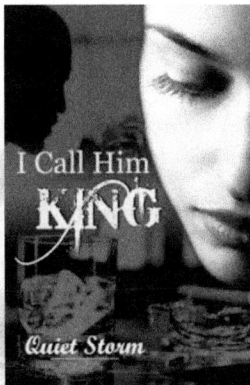

BATTERED SECRETS:
Men of Domestic Violence

Elva "Precious Love" Thompson

I Call Him KING
Quiet Storm

JAILED BY BLOOD:
INMATE 793175

Quiet Storm

"love jones"
the real version
from a poet's point of view

love jones\noun a strong
overwhelming desire for
someone.

Elva "Precious Love" Thompson

More Titles from
this Powerful,
Bestselling Author!!
www.EsquirePublications.com
Tel: 1-800-501-7640

PHF MAGAZINE

PHF MAGAZINE
Survivor Stories

PHF NEW YAL

PHF MAGAZINE
Don's Corner

PHF Magazine
www.PreciousHeartsFoundation.org
24/7 Helpline: 1-877-731-2210
Serving victims of domestic abuse, bullying & homelessness since 2009

Chapter *1*

Psalm 6:6 - I am worn out from groaning; all night long, I flood my bed with weeping and drench my couch with tears.

I get so angry that I just want to put the blame on him. It feels easier that way. I hate him for leaving us like he did, but I am glad he's gone. My heart is just confused right now with mixed emotions and feelings, with everything going through my mind all at once. I just want to scream until I can't scream anymore. I cried so much that I got headaches and my eyes were so red they swelled up. However I may feel, I will never ask, "Why me?" I never question mishaps that occur; I just chalk it up as being a part of life, of which there is a lot more to live, good and bad. I say to myself, "What doesn't kill me only makes me stronger," the typical words spoken. I just don't know how much stronger I can get.

My husband of fifteen years, without warning, just abandoned our three children and me, just walked out the door, as if he had the right because he concluded that he didn't love me anymore and fell in love with someone else and her children. What a blow that was. I later found out that this mystery woman was one of the many that he was cheating on me with, but he seemed to have a stronger rapport with her.

I had no idea that a person could have so many feelings all at once - being hurt, angry, confused. Finally, depression sets in and takes its toll. It was to the point that I didn't want to get out of bed in the morning. My children had to fend for themselves for a while. I never left my room and wouldn't have left my bed if it weren't for nature calling. I never ate and my kids would put plates of food by my bed. I just lay there as if there were no tomorrow. I was hopeless and felt helpless. Every day I thought, "What am I going to do?" "How am I going to take care of the girls?" I just wanted to die and take them with me. I didn't want to be a single mother.

My husband was only my second boyfriend. We were together since I was 15 years old. It was devastating, all right. My business of three years was dissolving because I had to sell my accounts to my independent contractors in order to pay the bills.

Shortly afterwards, my kids and I had to resort to seeking counseling because of the trauma and impact that was left when writing down our feelings was getting to be too much. It got to the point where we were writing three and four times a day, filling up legal notepads front and back. I felt like I lost everything. Our extremely residential, $250,000 home with back and front yards the size of basketball courts *(we were only one of two black families living in our neighborhood)*, my Ford Explorer and the Isuzu Rodeo I just bought Robert after trading in my convertible Mustang for it, and my mind. It was hard to keep and maintain focus on what needed to get done. I had to face reality, come to grip with everything, and get on the ball for my children's sake, as well as my own. They already lost their father; they didn't need to lose their mother too. All I've ever done and could do was pray. Pray to keep my sanity and pray for guidance with the lives of my children and life in general. Part of the hurt was Robert led me to believe that we were going to renew our wedding vows for our 10-year anniversary. We planned to renew every 5 years. I even went out and bought the girls' gowns and shoes only to have them returned. I was dreaming.

After a while, I finally got up, went to a lawyer, and filed for a divorce on the grounds of abandonment, along with filing for child support since my soon-to-be ex-husband flat out refused to help financially. His words were, "I don't live there anymore, I shouldn't have to help pay for anything." It made me sick to my stomach, especially knowing that we were about to be put out of this dream home. He didn't seem to care about the girls' welfare at all, or mine. I stayed up many nights wondering what my next move was going to be with a majority of our furniture and knick-knacks boxed up.

My home phone and business phone were ringing off the hook with employees wanting to know when their next account was going to take place. My email was so full that it took more than 15 minutes to download all the messages left. I knew that I couldn't tell them what was going on without them being concerned. In the state of mind that I was in, my girls and I were more important to me. All I could think about was leaving town. Just pick up and start over somewhere else. Some place where no one knew my situation or me. I would be a new face.

I got on the Internet and just started looking up apartments, but where? I knew that I wasn't going back up home to Pennsylvania. I would have felt like a failure even more by having to return home. There was nothing for me up there or anyone, except for Thomas Howard, my first love and boyfriend, but I didn't want to show up and begin interfering in his life, especially with all that I had on my plate. I was too embarrassed and I didn't exactly know how he would take to me after all these years. A part of me wanted to stay in Virginia, but the only nice parts to live were where we already were. Therefore, that was out of the question for sure. I had no idea.

Then, in the wee hours of the morning, a commercial came on television about www.bet.com. It was a chat line. I needed and desired to talk to someone. I figured why not. I had nothing else to lose. I got online and typed in the website and went to the chat room. I had no idea what to say, but it seemed that many people wanted to talk to me. I guess it was my name that drew them to me. Being a first timer, I didn't know enough to use a fake name, so I used my pen name, Precious as my screen name. I really didn't know what to expect so I answered every question that was asked to me, like "*How are you doing tonight?*" I didn't know what else to say except for the truth so I told them, "*Not so good.*" I went on to explain what was going on with me and before I knew it, men and women in the chat room were actually listening and being sympathetic.

Maybe this was what I needed now. It sure *felt* good. They were so supportive and offered all types of advice and encouragement. They made some of the cloudiness go away and brought a smile to my face. Then this one person in particular sent me an instant message with his phone number in it and said that if I wanted to talk one on one, to call him. Feeling as I did, again I thought, why not. I mean it was all in fun. I signed off after thanking everyone for their words of encouragement and kindness and decided to call this guy that seemed to care. I really needed the affection. I must have rung his number about three or four times and hung up for fear of actually calling another man besides my former husband of 15 years. I felt like I was cheating when in reality, I was not. Finally, I got up enough courage and called straight through and he answered with the sexiest baritone voice. Here I was calling and talking to someone I didn't know from Adam. He told me his name was Karl Grier. Karl, a 27-year-old Navy man stationed in Jacksonville, Florida, was originally from College Park, Georgia. After our conversation started going on about half an hour, he told me all about Georgia. Karl stated how children who kept their grades to an honor roll level have the opportunity of going to a college of their choice free. The first thing that came to my mind was that my girls were honor roll since kindergarten. They always brought home A's and B's, plus many famous black colleges were in Georgia. I was pretty confident that they would most definitely make something out of themselves down there and all the beautiful black culture they would be exposed to was exciting enough. I had no doubt in my mind and my faith in them was that strong. Karl also mentioned how my business could really take off with all the opportunity and potential there. He went on to tell me about how there were so many black owned businesses that grow each year for the better and if I didn't want to get started with my company right away that the jobs paid better in Georgia than in Virginia anyway. At this time, Karl had my total undivided attention. He stated how nice the people were and how it would be a great place for the girls to grow up. I thought well, my life is over in Virginia, so why not start over somewhere else and actually live life the way that I want to live it. I dreamed of what it would feel like to actually be able to get to know me again since after being with my husband for so long and having three children later on, I had lost my own identity. I wanted to discover me and get to know who I was and what I really wanted out of life...I was ready.

9

After sending pictures of me to Karl, he and I carried on for about three months. We would talk to each other three or four times a day, 7 days a week. He would call me before he left for work to tell me "*Have a good day*." He would call me from work at lunchtime to see how my day was going thus far. He would call me when he got home from work to let me know he was home. Karl actually would call me, being miles and miles away, just to let me know that he was going to have a few drinks with his Navy friends and would call me when he returned. We would talk sometimes until 2 or 3 o'clock in the morning, until one of us fell asleep on the phone. It was usually him first. I so much enjoyed his sincerity and sensitivity. That was something that I never had. It was to the point that Karl became my comfort and helped me to better deal with the situation at hand.

Shortly afterwards, I made the decision to make the move to Georgia. The next two weeks were filled with Karl and I being on the phone and the Internet at the same time, looking up apartments. He guided me to the "decent" places to live as far as the girls' were concerned. He helped me with the areas to stay away from and to find the areas that were good. Finally, we found a place in Marietta, Georgia. It was a 2 bedroom, 2 bathroom apartment for $765.00 per month. Marietta was an expensive area, but an excellent area for the kids and me to live in and for the girls to go to school. I also got a job starting the first week of June in Atlanta via the Internet. I e- mailed my resume to a company there and two days later, they called me and asked how soon I would be relocating there. I knew that I had to get on the ball then. In so little time, I had a new job and a new apartment. I needed to make this move quickly because everything seemed to be falling into place. However, my job was starting below what I was generating from running my own business, but it was still in my field. Now I was the employee, but at least I was still at home working and could be there for the girls when they got out of school.

CHAPTER 2

Genesis 24:42 - "When I came to the spring today, I said, 'LORD, God of my master Abraham, if you will, please grant success to the journey on which I have come.

I made plans four days before Mother's Day to fly to Georgia to get a good look at what our new surroundings would be like in our neighborhood. I also had to get a dry run of where I had to go to meet my new employer. Before I left, I made sure that the girls were safely in the care of my mother, who encouraged me to move on. She also made a call ahead of time to a first cousin I had that lived in Atlanta to let him know that I was coming down for those few days so he could be on the lookout for me to take me around. It was all so convenient and falling into place. I felt it was such a blessing. To make my trip even sweeter, I informed Karl of the days that I was going to be in Georgia and he made plans to meet me there. I thought finally, I am going to meet Karl Grier face to face. He saw a picture of me, but I never saw him. I was quite nervous, but at the same time, excited and looking forward to it. I mean, here I was getting ready to meet a man who I actually met online. I know I flipped my wig. I told my girlfriend Janet about it and she wasn't too pleased, but I justified it with "Hey, look at it like a blind date." She also informed me to be careful because my heart was far from being healed. Janet and my sister Rolonda were the only two that knew of my meeting Karl. I had too much going on with taking care of business with the new job and apartment. Even though I was nervous, I never felt fear in his regard. I couldn't wait to finally have the chance of meeting my confidant, my special friend.

When I arrived in Atlanta, my cousin Keith met me at the airport. We went over to his place and reminisced for a while and then he took me to my hotel suite after making plans for him to pick me up the next day to do the dry run of my new job and apartment. After he dropped me off to my suite, I can remember smiling and saying to myself, "Your heeeeerrrreeee!" I was too excited and kept trying to picture what Karl would look like, trying to put his wonderful voice and personality with an appearance. After I had a chance to soak in what little I could see of Georgia from my suite balcony, I felt comfort and had peace of mind. I then took a long hot bubble bath and pampered myself with sweet scents from candles that I had brung along in my suitcase and played my nice contemporary jazz that took me to another place of comfort every time I listened to it. All that was missing was the wine, but I hadn't touched alcohol in over 5 years and if I had just a sip of any kind, especially wine, I know I would have been through for the evening. I noticed the time getting by me and I didn't want to be caught in the tub and have Karl knocking on the door, so I hurried it up a bit and got dressed. Karl already knew exactly what hotel suite I was going to be in (and the room number) since he insisted that I call him as soon as my plane landed.

An hour later, I heard a knock on the door. When I opened it, there stood a tall, medium-build, caramel-colored handsome brotha whose looks were as wonderful as his voice. He was dressed in a tan colored suit with broad shoulders, very well groomed with his Navy faded haircut, and well kept facial hair. He greeted me with, "Hello Precious." I was speechless for the first few seconds just inhaling the moment of actually seeing him for the first time. While Karl unpacked his suitcase, I asked him if he was hungry, since I had ordered pizza and hot wings before he came. We ate and talked about what we both had to do the next day. Listening to him talk, I remember thinking to myself, "I can't believe he's here. I can't believe I'm here with him." It was definitely a new experience, but very enjoyable.

As we conversed, time began to leave us and we decided to get more comfortable by slipping into our bedclothes. I went into the bathroom to change into my nightgown. After I came out of the bathroom, Karl was already dressed down to his black silk boxers. He had already pulled back the covers and had his back turned towards me, surfing the radio station for the "quiet storm" until he found "I Wanna Know" by Joe. He then turned around and stood still in his tracks and just stared at me and said, "You truly are beautiful, you know that?" I received the response that I had hoped for and more.

He had no idea how much those words meant since it was so long ago that I had anyone say anything like that to me. A lump formed in my throat and my eyes swelled with tears. As my voice quivered "Thank you," Karl walked over to me, cupped my face with both hands, and wiped away a teardrop with his thumb running down my cheek and gently lifted my face to meet his and kissed me softly on the lips. Then he held me and squeezed me tightly and more tears began to flow. He whispered in my ear and said, "It's going to be all right." After I calmed down, we sat on the bed and talked until 2:30 A.M. We talked about the reason for my tears and the reason why I was in Georgia and the opportunities for the girls and myself. It was so refreshing, the thought of actually moving away to start a new life. I couldn't wait. Feeling our eyelids getting heavy, we laid down underneath the sheets with Karl embracing me. He was a gentleman in every way. I felt so comfortable and safe, not to mention grateful that he didn't try anything. I slept like a baby in his arms.

That morning, we woke up around 11:00 A.M., still in the same position as when we first lied down. We greeted each other with "Good morning" and Karl gave me a kiss on the cheek and held me even tighter. Even though we both had business to take care of, neither one of us wanted to break our moment of comfort, so we stayed in bed a little longer and drifted back off to sleep until after 3:00 P.M. I called my cousin to pick me up and Karl called his brother to pick him up so he could spend time with his family. Shortly after, my cousin arrived and he took me on a tour of downtown Atlanta. I was amazed at how huge the buildings were and the traffic was unbelievable. The more I saw, the more anxious I was to move there. I couldn't wait to get back to Virginia so I could tell the girls all about what I'd seen of Georgia so far. We were definitely going to start a new life together and live it to the fullest.

After seeing the whereabouts of my new job, we headed over to our new apartment to pay the deposit, first month's rent, sign the lease, and get my keys. Ahhh, the keys to our new place, just my girls and me. I felt even more independent and so in charge of my life. I had nothing but positive thoughts flowing through my mind. I couldn't stop smiling. I also couldn't wait to get back to the hotel with hopes of Karl being there. I had Keith take me to Burger King and drop me back off to the hotel suite. As I walked in, right away, I received Karl's lingering scent. He was lying across the bed asleep, looking just as adorable as he did when I first laid eyes on him. I woke him up with a kiss on the lips and I laid down beside him. I asked him why didn't his brother pick him up yet and he stated that he was really tired and that when he called his brother the first time, no one was home, so he decided to get some more rest. A few hours later, he didn't realize how late it had gotten, so Karl made another call to Mark to pick him up. An hour later, he arrived and he and Karl left to see their parents. Karl hadn't been home in a year. To pass the time away, I called home to see how the girls and my mother were doing and to let them know that I was okay and where Keith had taken me so far. My mother told me that Robert had been calling the house, but they just left him on the answering machine with his demands of wanting to speak to me. He then started coming around & banging on the door. Thank God I had the locks changed after he walked out. Since my mother wouldn't open the door for him, his banging got more intense.

Finally, after three days of Robert showing up and calling, he gave up. What nerve he had. He was the one who decided that he didn't want to be married to me anymore, now here he was thinking he had the right to speak to me. We didn't want him to know that I was out-of-town, let alone with plans to move to another state. He would definitely cause me trouble by trying to stop me from going via his fists. That was always his way of discussion. There were many days and nights of physical and verbal abuse I endured from him. It was always over his infidelities. The last straw for me was when he had a baby by another woman that he used to work with while we were married. He never asked for a blood test, even though she was also sleeping with two siblings, several other people on the job, and the office manager. At that time, anything that I had left by way of feelings for him was completely gone. I felt drained. I only stayed in my marriage for the sake of our children. I honored my vows and I never went outside my marriage.

12

After talking with my mother and assuring her that I was fine, I spoke with the girls and they wanted to know when I was coming home, even though they already knew this before I left. I guess it was their way of saying that they missed me. I missed them too and couldn't wait to get back to get my hugs and kisses from them. I didn't want to tell them about the apartment as of yet. I wanted to surprise them when I got back with the keys. I promised them when I left that I was coming back with a job and a place for us to live. Shortly after conversing back and forth with the girls and my mother, we ended the conversation with, "I love you." Feeling a bit fatigued, I lied across the bed and fell asleep. I didn't wake up until the blue sky was gone and the stars were out. At this time, I wondered where Karl was and if he was coming back since some of his luggage was still in the room. It was getting late, so I took a shower, slipped into my bedclothes and went to bed. Around 1 A.M., the phone rang. It was Karl. He had been hanging out with his brother and their friends, drinking all day and all night. He said that he wanted to come back to the room, but wanted to wait until sunup because he had a bit too much to drink.

I reminded him that I was leaving to go back to Virginia that morning. He replied with, "I know and I'm sorry, but I will get over there to see you before you leave." Karl had already asked his brother if he could borrow his car, but Mark was reluctant because he had to be to work at 5:00 A.M. that morning and didn't want to take a chance on Karl not being back on time, so he refused. Karl was very apologetic and asked if I was angry with him, but how could I be. I mean he wasn't my boyfriend. He was a beginning to a new friendship. I asked him if he enjoyed himself, and he replied that he had. I told him that I would see him in the morning, I turned out the light and I went to bed.

Morning came and my flight was set to take off at 11:42 A.M. Keith called me to let me know to be ready and down in the lobby at 11:15. As I was packing, all I could think about was Karl, hoping that he would be able to make it to see me before my flight took off for home. At 11:00 AM, the phone rang and it was Karl greeting me with, "Happy Mother's Day." I said, "Thank you" and asked if he was on his way. He replied with, "I'll be there in 5 minutes." Unfortunately, he was 5 minutes too late. Keith came a little earlier as the service desk informed me that he was downstairs waiting. I tried to stall a bit, but I couldn't miss my flight, so I left the hotel door unlocked for Karl to come in to retrieve the rest of his belongings. As Keith and I left the hotel parking lot, Karl and I caught each other's eye as we were passing by.

CHAPTER 3

2 Samuel 7:6 - I have not dwelt in a house from the day I brought the Israelites up out of Egypt to this day. I have been moving from place to place with a tent as my dwelling.

After my plane landed back at the Norfolk Airport, my mother and daughters were there to greet me. I was so glad to see them. We drove back home to Virginia Beach and my mother informed me that she would be moving back up home to Harrisburg, Pennsylvania to live, but that she would make sure the girls and I were safe and on our way to Georgia first. I assured her that everything would be fine and told her what I saw of Georgia and the apartment and that we were ready to move in the first week of June. I started my new job one week after. With the house nearly packed up, we were almost ready to go. After getting home, Robert called. I told him that we were moving, but I didn't tell him exactly where. Of course, he assumed that we were moving locally. I gave him no other inclinations of anything other than what he already thought. I didn't want him to know that we were moving out-of-state. I couldn't afford any delays; everything was right on track. The girls already knew to keep everything hush-hush. I informed their schools that we would be moving, but without their father, and that he was not to take them out of school. I told them that we were getting a divorce, but I didn't go into detail on why. The looks on their faces were filled with sympathy for me, but they just didn't know how happy I was inside. I couldn't wait to get to Georgia.

The days were getting close and the clock was winding down to be Georgia bound. I was waiting for my brother Savon to drive down from Pennsylvania. He was the mover that was going to drive my rental truck to Georgia for me while I followed in my Explorer. The time was getting later and later and I was getting more and more frustrated and scared because I knew that when daylight came, Robert would come to the house to harass me. I just wanted to be out of there before he even had a chance to show up. Frustrated as ever, I called Karl, who flew back to his barracks in Florida. He answered and asked me what was wrong after hearing the quivering in my voice. I told him that I didn't think we would make it to Georgia because my brother had not arrived yet. Karl assured me that everything was going to be all right. He knew that I was just upset and anxious at the same time and told me not to worry. He even offered to have a few of his Navy buddies stationed at the Norfolk Naval Base to come and help me load up the moving truck, but I refused it being that I didn't know how to explain Karl's friends to my daughters, let alone explain exactly who Karl was and how I had met him. I wasn't ready to spring nothing like that on my babies. All they had ever seen me with was their daddy and our situation was devastating enough so I didn't want to add on more mess to the pile.

Well, 11 P.M. rolled around and finally, Savon pulls up... thank goodness. I greeted him at the door with a hug and a big thank you for his help. We started loading up the truck. By that time, my sister Rolonda and her boyfriend Sammy were about to leave. Rolonda stayed with me until my mother was all packed to move back to Pennsylvania. My other brother Winston and his friends had moved our mother. After Savon showed up, Rolonda and Sammy helped move a few loads of furniture onto the truck, but it was getting late and she had already stayed with me for my last few days in Virginia, which was very much appreciated. She and Sammy went back home to Williamsburg after Rolonda and I embraced and cried. She was so sorry for my situation, but at the same time, told me of her belief that my daughters and I were making the right move and we were going to do just fine in Georgia. I didn't want to let her go, but she had to go and so did I. We took our last look at each other for a while and departed. Then to my surprise, my best friend and only girlfriend Janet had pulled up in front of the house after having just got off work and stayed with us until 6 A.M., which was the time we finished loading all that we could fit on the truck. For the rest of my furniture, Janet had her father come to put the rest of my items in his garage.

Janet took us to the highway to see us off. Before we got started on the road, we pulled over to the roadside to say our last goodbyes. Janet and I just embraced and cried. She even gave me $60 to help out with gas. Now this was a girl that did not part with money, but she was a true friend indeed. I was going to miss her most out of my friends from Virginia, besides Rolonda. Janet was always there for me, ever since we met back in 1994 at a local hospital where we both worked. She was there for me when I called crying on the phone about my husband beating on me and cheating on me. Janet was there. On most days, when I couldn't come to work because of being bruised and having black eyes from Robert, Janet would work my hours even after having just finished her 8 hour shift. She was sympathetic to what I was going through and she was the only one that I could tell about all the drama that was going on within my household. All of those thoughts flashed through my mind when we held each other. All I could do was look at her. Janet kept repeating herself, with tears in her eyes, saying "It's going to be all right." I was too teary-eyed and choked up to speak, so I gave her my last hug, and got back into my vehicle. Savon followed in the moving truck, and we headed to Georgia.

CHAPTER 4

Jeremiah 46:5 - What do I see? They are terrified, they are retreating, their warriors are defeated. They flee in haste without looking back, and there is terror on every side," declares the LORD.

Shortly after being on the road for about three hours into our drive, we stopped to fill up on gas and to get something to eat. Savon and I were both tired after being up all night loading furniture onto the truck and now we were making a 10-hour run from VA to GA, but we had a plan and we were on a mission. We had to continue. We filled up our tanks, got something to eat for everyone, stretched our legs a little more, and then headed back onto the highway for Georgia. While continuing on our journey, I talked to the kids about leaving their friends, school, and their dad. I thought maybe they had some bottled up feelings they wanted to release. To my surprise, they were just as excited as I was about leaving and starting over. They even reassured me that everything was going to be all right and that we were going to make it just fine without "him", as they now referred to their dad. I could sense their bitterness towards him and I couldn't blame them at all. He chose to walk out and leave his family for another woman and her children instead of being a man.

The whole way to Georgia, I couldn't stop thinking about everything that had happened in my life with Robert since the day we met. It was worse than a nightmare, but at the same time, even in my disbelief, I was happy. I felt like it was the right thing to do or the Lord wouldn't have made it possible for us to get this far. Talk about having mixed emotions. My mind was going back and forth. Deep down, I always knew that eventually, Robert and I weren't going to be together forever. I knew this time would come, but I just didn't know how it was coming. Whenever Robert was doing wrong, he stopped wanting to go to church and had no desire to want to touch me intimately. He did this every time he cheated, which I can't even count on both hands. Then there was the devastating, unforgettable baby he made during our marriage with a woman that he carried on with for over a year, on and off, at his then job as a mover for a national moving company. Dana was 4 years older than Robert. She was a divorced mother of three children that her ex-husband was awarded custody of. I first met Dana when I would bring Robert lunch. She looked like the "homely-type." She was the first one to greet me and you know what they say about the first to greet you. She was the epitome of that saying and then some. I didn't receive a very good vibe from her. Every day, I would bake Robert and his fellow employees' cookies or brownies to take to them. Every time I drove up, there was Dana in his face. Of course, she was the first to spot me pulling up, so she would come to the car to greet me with a phony smile, speaking highly of Robert. Something just didn't feel right.

Shortly afterwards, Robert told me to stop coming to his job and that he was going out for lunch from now on. Right then I knew, but what could I say, I had no real proof. I just prayed to the Lord to show me what was going on, to give me some kind of sign. A few days later, my phone rang and it was a fellow employee of Robert's. Her name was Carla. Carla was the "fed up-type" of woman that has been through it all. When she called, she informed me that she did not want to upset me, but that she thought I was a nice person and hated the fact that this husband of mine was stepping out on me with what she referred to as a "trashy skank." Carla told me that everyone at the job was talking about how they would go on long lunches together and at times, Robert would eat and drink after Dana. Right then, my heart dropped because I knew that this was the sign that I asked for of the Lord. I thanked her for her concern, but I didn't let on that I believed her right away, even though I did. When Robert came home, I asked him who he had lunch with and he said, "The guys," but he couldn't even look me in the eyes just to tell me that. I didn't want to confront him about Dana or tell him about the phone call I received. I wanted to wait a little.

A few days went by and I decided to show up at his job, without his permission, at lunchtime just to see what "guys" he was going to lunch with. When I got there, all of the "guys" were at work eating their lunch outside, so I proceeded to wait for Robert in my car and he pulled up with Dana in her car. The looks on their faces were unexplainable. It was as if they had seen a ghost. The guys just laughed and Dana walked away. Robert came over to the car and screamed at me, asking what I was doing there and I told him that I wanted to surprise him, but it looked like I was the one that got the surprise. This made him very angry and he told me that he would go to lunch with whomever he chose. It was as if he had no shame in his game.

At that moment, he had given me all the information I needed. Days after, the phone calls and hang-ups began. When I would *69 the number, it traced back to the vicinity of where Dana lived, but there were a lot of different phone booths that surrounded her place of residence. I knew the first three digits of the telephone number from where she lived. She would call our home and hang up on me whenever I answered. That was his queue to leave and come to her apartment. He would leave, but not before starting a no nonsense argument with me to justify his storming out the door and not being seen until he had to go to work the next day. The only time I would see him would be at 6A.M. to shower and change into his fresh work clothes. I had to take pictures of the kids before they went to school just so he could see what they looked like. He would be on his mission again while I was left taking care of his bedridden father, who had Alzheimer's disease. Robert had to drive 6 hours from Virginia to Pennsylvania to pick his father up and bring him down to Virginia to live with us.

Out of fifteen children, all residing in Pennsylvania and a few living in the same house as the father, they all refused to take care of him. The one that did as much as she could was Dena, a stepchild to his father. Robert had the nerve to tell me that his youngest sister Leslie, who was the same age as myself, had to go on with her life and shouldn't be stuck taking care of their own dad. What a nonsense statement, as if my life was over. I already had to take care of our 6-month-old daughter, and our oldest had just gotten out of the hospital two weeks prior from having brain surgery to remove a tumor at the age of 5. The tumor was removed, but it left her with diabetes insipidus, hypopituitary thyroidism, and petit mal seizures. The doctors say that she was born with this tumor, but that it could not be detected at birth. She has been taking medication ever since. At the time, she was taking a total of 22 pills day and night, but now has been narrowed down to six pills a day, which is a blessing, along with her not ever having to deal with special education or losing her good sense. She is a normal 13-year-old now that is slightly over her normal weight because of the medicine. I remember when the tumor first took its toll on her and we rushed her to the hospital, the doctor gave her a CT scan of the head and stated that she had a tumor. They said that the tumor was growing as she was growing. I thought I would die on the spot. I thought to myself, "Not my child." Right away, they scheduled the operation. She was in the hospital for two weeks straight. At the time, I didn't know anything was going on with Robert and Dana and she showed up at the hospital. Along with her in our presence were my mother and a few pastors that were sent by my oldest brother Wallace, who was a pastor of his church in Illinois. He sent a prayer chain from Illinois, to Virginia, California, and Pennsylvania.

One of the pastors there informed my brother that they had hoped that Robert's affair was over because he saw a sign over his head that pertained to just that. On top of all of that, our middle child, who was 3, had the chicken pox and gave it to the youngest and the oldest. The girls' all had the chicken pox at the same time. My Cesarean section hadn't had a chance to heal properly and I was still working full-time and going to college full-time in the evening. All I could do was pray. When he brung his father to our home, I remember thinking to myself as I looked at his dad, "What no good kids he had." When his dad first met Robert's mother, whom he never married, she already had 10 kids by 3 different men, but being the wonderful man that his father was, he stayed with her and helped her raise them and had 5 more with her. I always liked Robert's father.

17

He was a quiet man that only spoke when necessary and when he did, he always made good sense. I admired him. Hard to believe that Robert was his son, being as rotten as he turned out to be. I guess he got that from his mother, who died a month before his father did. She was a force of evilness. I have never in my 31 years on this earth ever encountered such an evil woman. She told Robert, "You know light-skinned girls are trifling." She told him that right after Robert introduced us, but he never defended me. She even told him that our oldest daughter wasn't his, and then she told him she was, and then she told him that our middle child wasn't his either, then she changed her mind about that too. As for our youngest daughter, she didn't have the pleasure of being around too much to make a ludicrous remark like that. She told him not to marry me, but to marry his son's mother, who was on welfare and has been ever since their son was born 16 years ago. His mother never liked me because I never kissed her ass unlike his brother's girlfriends and wives. She never liked them either. She didn't like anyone that her ten boys were with. She said nasty, horrible things about them as well. On her deathbed, she told Robert that I was a good woman and she was glad he married me. What a crappy line. She just saw that she couldn't break me like she did the other girlfriends and wives. I turned out to be the opposite of all the negative statements and comments she claimed I would be. His brother's girlfriends and wives would talk about her badly, but if she were in front of them, they would bow down to her and kiss her ass. I was never one to do that type of nonsense. I just stayed to myself, laid back in the cut, and listened to their phony asses. What a bunch of silly insecure cackling hens. They just didn't know that if I wouldn't have had any kids by Robert, I would have been gone after meeting his mother. I stayed for the sake of my children and took my vows seriously.

I ended up having to quit my job to take care of his father for the past two months because outside help would have been too expensive. Robert's father's ill health took its toll and he died on the fourth of July with me at his bedside. Robert wasn't even in the room. He was on the phone with Dana, and when I told him that his father had just passed, he called his siblings to make the funeral arrangements. Everybody acted as if they didn't have any money to help, so it all boiled down to us having to use our rent money to pay for the expenses. His siblings promised to pay him back...not us, but him and they never have. He still owes over $400 to the funeral home in order to get his dad's death certificate. Being that his father was a Veteran, they shipped his body back up home free of charge where his funeral took place. I read a little poem I wrote in remembrance of him at the funeral and the snickering was ridiculous. I tried to block their ignorant asses out of my mind and remembered that I was doing it for the father. Afterwards, his family talked about how great Robert was for taking care of their father and working at the same time. I thought I would die after hearing that. I said to myself, "Lord, please help me," then that's when Robert intervened and told them that I was the one that took care of their dad. I was the one that quit my job and wiped the feces from his behind. I cleaned up his bedwetting and gave him baths, fed him, and dressed him. I was the one that kept him well-groomed with hair cuttings and beard shavings, lifting him up off the floor and back onto the bed, which would happen too often for me after having a Cesarean 6-month old. However, he failed, of course, to tell them that I did all this while he was out whoring around with Dana making a baby, never being home and when he was, he would beat the hell out of me in a drunken rage. I wanted so much to tell them what was going on, but it really didn't matter because they still looked at him and thanked him for taking their father in. Not one of them said thank you to me, except for Dena. I cried with rage inside and couldn't open my mouth to anyone, except to pray. I despised being around those people and dreaded every millisecond of it. All I wanted to do was disappear with my children.

After the funeral, we went back home to Virginia where Robert started his "thing" back with Dana. Having no shame in his game, he became even more careless with his infidelity. The kids told me that while I was in school at night studying for my new career, he would have her in our home, in our bed where they saw and heard her voice. He claimed they were only kids and they didn't know what they were talking about, but I trusted my girls' and it didn't matter that they were 4 and 6 at the time. They described her to me, down to her blonde hair and her sailor mouth. They even described the color of her car that was parked in our back driveway. I thought about leaving, but where could I go? I had family, but this was a mess that I got myself into and I didn't want to turn to them. This was my marriage and I had to trust in God to answer my prayers, so I kept my mouth shut and followed where the Lord led me. I switched my college hours to morning and got a part-time job in the field I was going to school in.

Then just when things were going well for me career-wise, here came the devil again with Robert's self-centered, no reason to be conceited sister Victoria coming to live with us until her military husband and their two spoiled rotten, back talking children found available housing. Robert really showed his ass in their presence with down talking me in front of them and Victoria letting me know that she didn't care for me either. She would laugh so loud at every degrading thing Robert spoke about me, but Brian, Victoria's husband would never crack a smile. I appreciated that and by him doing that, he let me know that he could see what I was going through. This sister in particular was just like having his mother living in my house. It was worse than a nightmare every day they were there. Brian was nice, but he wasn't allowed to speak to me. I translated that to be that Victoria was insecure. I didn't sweat it. I just looked at him thinking to myself, "I really feel sorry for you brotha." She was a non-cooking, fast food dinner making, don't want to break a nail, broke down want to be diva. She was a rude, ignorant, sarcastic, brainless heffa that was one year younger than Robert but had finally graduated from high school a year before me. Robert is five years older than I am which means he graduated in 1984 and she should have graduated in 1985, but was too stupid and didn't get out until 1987. Victoria was four years older than her husband Brian; he and I were the same age. She dug her claws into him quick, a young military man, so she wouldn't have to work and married him right away. She had to; she was already pregnant with their first child at the time. He had to marry her before the baby was born.

Leslie, the younger sister, did the same thing. She had already had a child by a military guy, but he wasn't a fool and bunked out on her, but still took care of his son. Then she got pregnant by his cousin and had to marry him before their baby was born. She actually walked down the aisle waddling. Her husband Arthur was a nice person too. He wasn't allowed to talk to me either, but he was pretty level headed and talked to me anyway. I felt sorry for that brotha too. Arthur and Brian were really nice guys, but got caught like I did and stayed for the sake of their children. They too knew the strangeness of this family. We would talk to each other with our eyes by giving stares whenever Robert or one of his family members said something off the wall, which was often, but we never spoke a word to one another about it.

After Victoria and Brian finally moved out into their military housing, the devil just wouldn't let up on me. Next came his crack addicted Brother George. This guy was a doozy and a half. When he wasn't out smoking crack half the night, he was in jail. Robert was giving him $20's, $50's, and $100's at a time, supporting his habit. This was taking from our home when I had to borrow money from my mother to help pay rent. All I could tell her was that we ran short for the month. She never asked questions, but I could tell that she sensed something wasn't right and she wasn't too happy about it, but respected me enough not to get into my business. George was a major influence on Robert, as were all his siblings. He encouraged him to be with Dana and actually told him to leave me because our kids were almost grown and the baby he and Dana made together needed him more. Our girls were six and under. It didn't take much for Robert. He took his brother's advice and left us, and he and George stayed over Dana's house for a few days.

19

I decided I had more than enough of his family and his nonsense, so I went to look for Robert in the area that I knew Dana lived. To my surprise, I happened to see Robert's car parked in the lot of Burger King, but Robert wasn't there. George had his car. When I approached George about Robert's whereabouts, he came at me and began putting his hands around my neck. The girls' were in my car crying and screaming, banging on the window. Then a security guard came over and asked if there was a problem. Before I could get myself together to speak a word, George told him no, that he and I, who he referred to as his "girlfriend", were having an argument. I was so devastated and hurt for my children having to witness this that I just got back in my car crying and went home apologizing to the kids the whole way. When we got home, Robert came walking in the door twenty minutes later with no words to speak. I proceeded to tell him what his brother had done to me and his reply was "I told George not to put his hands on you." That's all he had to say about that.

At that moment, I told Robert that I wanted a divorce. Before I could finish the word, he charged at me with flying fists, knocked me down, and began kicking me, yelling for me to get up. I tried crawling to the other room because the girls had now witnessed yet another horrifying experience. I begged him to not do this in front of the girls, but he commenced to calling me a fat bitch and said that I got on his fucking nerves and how much he hated me. I wanted to die that night, like many other nights, and take my children with me. Needless to say, Robert ended up leaving that night to go back to Dana's and took my car keys with him. While he was gone, I apologized to the girls and put them to bed. I finally decided to tell someone what was happening and called my girlfriend Janet and told her what was going on with me. She was shocked and angry. Janet had just finished working an 8 hour shift from 3 P.M.- 11. P.M., but turned right back around and worked my shift for me from 7 A.M.- 4 P.M. I couldn't go to work like that. Janet helped me out with working herself like this, back to back, until my marks were almost invisible. Afterwards, Robert finally came home with George. They sat up half the night drinking and reminiscing about their parents. As if the incidents between the three of us never took place. All I could do was pray as before and I cried myself to sleep many nights. I had wishful thoughts of the girls and I getting into a car accident and dying. That way, we would be together and have no more worries or heartaches.

The next day, Robert went to work and took George and dropped him off somewhere. I spent that morning getting the girls ready for pre-school and elementary school, tending to the baby, and trying to nurse my wounds at the same time. The girls would look at me, as young as they were with tears in their eyes, and say, "I'm sorry Mommy." All I could do was hug them, tell them I love them, and apologize to them for having to live this way. I promised them that I would try to make things better, but I don't think I believed that could happen myself. I just wanted to give them some kind of reassurance. That evening, after being off work for over 6 hours, Robert finally came home, but without George. He said that George was in jail for robbing a bank. It just seemed like the nightmare just wasn't going to end. I knew that with George being in jail, more of our money was going out the window. George would call collect so many times on a daily basis, sometimes two or three times a day, that it ran our phone bill up to over $200 because Robert kept accepting the charges. It later turned out to be mistaken identity on George's part, but that didn't change him. He still abused drugs and alcohol. Robert finally got fed up with him freeloading and told him he had to leave.

George ended up going back to Pennsylvania and no sooner than him getting back in town, he was put in jail again. This time for non-child support payments for his four kids, all girls, by two different women.

CHAPTER 5

Exodus 15:2 -"The LORD is my strength and my defense; he has become my salvation. He is my God, and I will praise him, my father's God, and I will exalt him.

As the months went by, Robert started staying home more. Turns out that Dana broke it off with him and filed for custody of their daughter, for who he pays no child support for to this day. He threatened her that if she ever filed, he was going to take the little girl away from her. The child was born with lung problems and learning disabilities. To my knowledge, at this time, Robert has never visited that child. At this point in my life, experiencing the pain and turmoil Robert inflicted upon me, I had no love for him. He drained me. I despised hearing him breathe. All I could think about was finishing college and making life better for my girls. I had plans and I was on a mission. So I endured more pain and stayed for the sake of my children. I tried to avoid arguments by agreeing with him, even when he was wrong. I listened to him vent about Dana and his other infidelities. It was hard to swallow at first, but I dealt with it and to my surprise, it made me stronger. I had no more jealous feelings about him being with other women because I no longer cared for him. It took away my fear of him because he allowed me to see how weak he really was. While he was venting, he was looking at me as a "good person" to listen to him after all that he's put me through. However, I was looking at him thinking to myself, "Keep it coming brotha because the more you talk, the stronger I get." More and more, I saw his real face. The face of a momma's boy and a coward.

After finally graduating from college, I worked full-time in my field. I appreciated the job, but felt it wasn't enough for me. I wasn't satisfied. There was something else out there that was waiting for me. I could feel it in my bones, but I just didn't know what it was I was feeling until I took that leap of faith. I quit my job, picked up some old equipment from the employer's warehouse before I quit and decided to start my own business. I went downtown and applied for my business license. To save money, I made brochures and business cards on my home computer. To gain clientele, I did a lot of cold calling straight out of the phonebook. Of course I had many, many turn downs, but I didn't give up. It just motivated me to keep going until I got what I wanted to hear...a yes, finally a yes. I was officially a small business owner, of my own medical transcription service, working out of the comfort of my own home. It was truly a blessing and a new beginning. Of course, my small success had to come with a price. Robert didn't like the idea at all. He down talked it and told me on many occasions to just give it up because I wouldn't make any money, but I had more faith than that.

This was something that I had to do and I was not going to allow him to discourage me. At the time, with this one client, I was only making approximately $50-$75 per week. I was still happy because it was something that I was doing on my own.

Shortly after about 5 months into my new home-based business, word-of-mouth began to help generate more clientele for me. Robert told his siblings what I was doing and of course their negativity, or should I say jealousy, was made known by Victoria telling him that I wasn't really working, that I was just laying around all day while he was working hard outside our home. He believed her by asking me what exactly is it that I do all day, so I showed him by typing some reports in his presence. For once, I convinced him, but it wasn't long before she came up with another negative statement that my "so-called business" wasn't making any money, which was none of her business. However, he took it to that level again and asked to see the invoices I billed my clients. Talk about being angry and humiliated. I showed him, which at that time, fluctuated from $50-$75 per week to $200-$350 per week.

As my business was going well for me, Robert managed to put a hold on it by getting himself in trouble with the law. It seemed like there was something new going on with him every year. This was more of a strain on our marriage. After he and Dana fell out, he left that moving company job and decided to use his computer repair diploma he received a year before I graduated from college in an entry-level position with a well-known computer company doing inventory of computer parts. About a year into his position, he and two other employees were under investigation. They had a scam going on where Robert would allow these two guys to take laptop computers out of inventory and sell them. Robert wouldn't record the laptops in inventory and receive monetary gifts to keep quiet. Well you know that someone had to open their mouth and brag about the scheme and when they did, the shit hit the fan. Robert was so good at keeping his mouth shut that he didn't even tell me what was going on until after he got busted.

Robert had resigned with that company and began working for another company, but this time he moved up to being an actual technician. However, being that they were working under a government contract with the old employer, the NIS got involved with the investigation and Robert's past caught up to him. I was glad that he had gotten himself into some mess, thinking he would finally learn his lesson about doing wrong, but I was pissed off that the girls and I had to suffer because of it. He ended up getting probation for three years and house arrest for six months. He was only allowed to go to work and come straight home. Instead of thanking the Lord that his new job kept him, he continued to do wrong. He was drinking even more and commenced to beating the hell out of me. All I could do was pray and strive to keep my business going. It was my ticket out. After being told that Dana helped him financially with paying bills because I had to quit to take care of his father, I thought to myself, he will never catch me off guard like that again. The ignorance of him and his family motivated me even more.

With Robert being on house arrest, that meant that his family members would come over to the house to visit. I couldn't stand it, especially seeing Victoria and her spoiled ass kids. They all made a joke out of him being on house arrest by saying things like, "I know you will be glad to get out the house so you can breathe." I took it as being a shot at me, but I brushed it off and thought that this was one time that they couldn't put the blame on me like they did when he was cheating with other women, having a baby by Dana, and beating on me. They actually stated that I must have done something to make him do all that he had done to me. However, I was mistaken. They managed to put his house arrest on me too. They told him that if I had a "real job" he wouldn't have had to take money in order to pay bills. They just didn't know the facts. Robert ate that up. He liked being the center of attention with them. He could do no wrong in their eyes, even when he was wrong. I never even knew what he was doing until he actually got busted and I never saw any "extra" money. I paid the bills; he only contributed less than half. I was truly living a nightmare. All I could do was pray like every other day of my life spent with him.

With Robert being on house arrest, it was taking a toll on our marriage. I wasn't use to having him come straight home from work and actually staying. Different probation officers would pay a visit to make sure he was abiding by the rules. This made Robert very irritable because he wasn't use to being home straight after work either, then having authority figures stopping by at anytime to make sure he is doing the right thing just wasn't a good thing for him. It was killing him inside, which meant more pain inflicted upon me. This one time in particular, Robert had more to drink than he could handle and my mother just happened to visit that evening and witnessed what I believe she suspected was going on all along. Robert dared to put his hands on me in front of my mother. My heart was hurting for her more than the blows he was giving me. I hated that she had to witness her youngest daughter in this type of predicament.

22

We managed to push him out the door of our home and she ordered me to call the police, but I couldn't. I saw the look in his eyes when she gave the order and I just didn't want to deal with the consequences of the aftermath. So after my mother and Robert were pushing the door back and forth trying with her trying to keep him out and he trying to get back in, his strength out did her and he forced his way back in the door. Understandably, not being able to bare much more, mother left and took the girls with her for the evening. Robert just sat around and went channel surfing on the tube as if nothing happened. I ran into the bathroom to try and fix my glasses that he busted the lens out of with a blow to my face. I had a black eye for at least two weeks and a busted, bloody bottom lip. My hatred for him grew and grew. I was so upset that my mother had to witness this. I couldn't imagine how it made her feel.

At this point, I didn't care too much about what I was feeling because it was nothing new. He had always beaten me ever since I was 16. We started courting when I was 15 years old, but the beatings began after we had our first daughter and continued on thereafter. I would take the kids' beatings. I knew how hard he hit me and I didn't dare want that pain instilled in my girls'. It was bad enough he would smack them upside their heads to "straighten them out", per Robert. When he would catch himself disciplining them, his way was always the belt or his hands, but I would intercede and tell him that I would take care of their punishment. This only made him angrier and according to him, it was grounds to beat me because he looked at it like I was telling him that he had no rights to his children. I took the beatings because by him hitting on me, it made him forget about his plans of punishment for the girls.

Later on in the evening, as soon as I could hear him snoring, I would slip out of bed and go into the girls' room and apologize to them. Sometimes, it would be after midnight that I would go in their rooms to apologize and they would wake right up as if they were expecting me. We whispered, trying to be careful not to wake Robert with our conversation and our tears. I tried explaining to them why he was angry, but I let them know that they did nothing wrong. My heart was crying inside, but I couldn't shed another tear in front of them. I had to be strong for them and for me. After our hugs and I love you's, I slipped back into bed and he would turn over and ask where I was. I told him I had to go to the bathroom. He would then put his arm across my chest and go back to his snoring. I despised his hands on me. I could remember thinking that if I didn't have any children by him, I would have been gone a long time ago. I only married him because of our children. I still remember the awful suggestion, not proposal, he gave. *"Since we already have kids, we might as well get married, so go ahead and call the justice of the peace and set it up."* I felt like shit. I thought to myself, "What the hell was that?" Needless to say, I called and "set it up" and on April 9, 1990, we were married. I can still remember the feeling that overwhelmed my spirit when he placed the ring on my finger. It wasn't a kind feeling at all, but I just felt like this had to be done for my children and I didn't want to live in sin any longer by shacking up with him. I couldn't help but to think, "What does my future hold being married to him?"

Around the time Robert was to get off probation, he had this one probation officer in particular, Mrs. Arlene Hill, that chose to speak to me when she came to visit instead of talking to him like she was supposed to. I wanted so much to let her know what type of person he really was, but I kept my mouth shut and just agreed with her compliments towards him and how nice of a man he seemed to be. It was like reading about those bad cops that treated their family like crap behind closed doors, but were outstanding citizens on the street and amongst their peers. I would look into her eyes and think to myself, "Please read my thoughts." It was useless; he had her fooled too. Three years had gone by and probation was finally over, but it wasn't soon enough for Robert. He couldn't wait to get out. He went back to his late night ventures and began seeing Dana again. Later on in the year, I found out that he told her that I was the cause of his probation.

CHAPTER 6

Psalm 55:10 - Day and night they prowl about on its walls; malice and abuse are within it.

The money I was making from my business wasn't enough for me to get to where I wanted to be in the business, so I went to work full-time back at the hospital and slowly, but surely, the business began to fade out. I just couldn't hold it down with working full-time during the day and sitting up half the night typing reports, then having to deal with the stress from Robert and raising my girls. It was too much being a mom, cook, housekeeper, wife, and punching bag. I sent my clients a resignation letter telling them my father died and I had to leave town. I always used my father as the "death in the family" excuse because he was never there for my siblings and me anyway. *When he did manage to come home, he was abusive to my mother and my siblings. With me being the youngest out of 8 children, I guess I was too little for him to beat on. My mother and father divorced when I was 2 years old, so he really wasn't a part of my life, but it wasn't that I didn't try to be a part of his. Whenever he felt like talking to me, he would get in touch with my oldest brother and ask him to ask me if he could have my number. I would tell my brother to give it to him because I was pleased that he wanted to talk to me. It never lasted long. My father would call and talk like he had sense, then he would turn the conversation around and began talking badly about my mother. Needless to say, this made me very angry, so I defended my mother and told him that if he can't call and talk to me about anything else other than bad mouthing my mother, then I did not want him calling me anymore. Shocked that I would talk to him like that, he sent a message to my oldest brother that he didn't think that I was his child because I didn't act anything like him. I was better off cutting ties with my father. He was never there anyway and my mother was always enough for me.*

Being back at the hospital to work made me even more miserable than being at home. I had to hire a baby sitter, an 18- year-old teenager that I later found out Robert had an affair with, and then I had to go through the horrible process of going through different sitters. No one was good enough for my babies and I had no help from Robert. All he had to do was get up and go. I was left stuck with having my job in jeopardy trying to find a babysitter. Finally, I managed to get a reliable sitter, someone less attractive to Robert and much older. I hated the idea that I had to give up the business. I tried to look at it as the business being on hold temporarily. Getting back into the groove of things at work, it didn't get much better at home. The beatings continued and my bruises began to show more. I tried to camouflage my bruises and black eyes with makeup, but it was obvious what was going on with me. However, no one ever said anything except for Janet. She would tell me that I had to do something about him and that he's going too far. She said that I needed to talk to someone besides her about what was going on, but I couldn't. Janet's meaning of talking to someone was to tell another brotha because she would say that Robert needed his ass kicked. She was right, but that would only make things worse for me and the girls at home.

As the months went by, I began to interact more with fellow employees. There was one employee named John Pierce. John worked in the operating room as a technician. He was unhappily married with an adopted son that was his wife's sister's child. She made the decision to give her son up at birth and John wanted to keep him in the family, so he stepped up to the plate and adopted him, which was the cause of his marriage being unhappy. He never had any biological kids of his own and his wife had a 14-year-old daughter from a previous marriage and didn't want any more children. John was to me the epitome of a man and a big hearted gentleman in every sense of the word. John was 11 years older than

ELVA "PRECIOUS LOVE" THOMPSON

I and kicked knowledge to me unlike any other. He was full of wisdom and every time he spoke, I was there to listen. John would come by my department everyday to say hello. He was such a sweet man to me. He was caring, sensitive, and understanding. I needed that. I desired to have that in my life.

Shortly afterwards, we would go to lunch together in the hospital cafeteria and talk about how our days were going, then about our home life. I think John knew that something wasn't right with me. He began noticing my bruises and would ask me about them. I was too embarrassed to answer him, so I would just look at him with a half smile and tell him that everything was okay. He didn't buy that and would not let up. Finally, he came right out and asked if my husband was beating on me. What could I say to that? Nothing. I just looked at him and broke down in tears. He held me and mumbled under his breath, "I knew it." At that moment, I felt relief. I told someone else like Janet had advised and it felt damn good.

A burden was lifted and I felt comfort with John…a real man that listened and understood my pain. John gave me a number to a law firm and told me to consult a lawyer and inquire about a divorce. I wasn't ready to do that just yet. I remembered the last time I tried to tell Robert that I wanted a divorce and he beat the hell out of me before I could get the whole word out, so that was totally out of the question. Plus, I didn't want to put my girls through that. I had no plan B to move on. Where would we go? I had this big hang up about not wanting to be a single mom. I didn't want to become a "statistic."

Shortly after, John and I began spending many more lunches together, but we would leave the hospital. Our lunches consisted of 30 minutes of talk, talk, talk. It wasn't long before fellow employees began talking amongst themselves in regards to our lunches together. Everyone knew that John and I were married, but it didn't matter to us what anyone thought or said because they were totally platonic and innocent lunches. John and I clicked and the chemistry between us was booming. The more we went to lunch together, the more we became attracted to one another. While sitting in John's vehicle, he asked if he could kiss me. I was completely surprised, but at the same time, glad that he had asked. I told him yes and he leaned over and kissed me in a way that I had never been kissed. Afterwards, I felt the guilt overwhelm me in such a way that I couldn't speak. I must have made John feel bad because he apologized and we drove back to the hospital in silence. I couldn't look at him. The rest of my day was filled with me being clumsy and silent. I couldn't even tell Janet what happened, but I think she knew something was up because whenever we were together, we were like two cackling hens, but not that day. She just whispered to me to be careful.

When I went home, fear came over me as if Robert knew what I had done. For the next few days, I couldn't go to work. I faked sickness. I didn't want to see John. It was hard to face him. All I could think about was what happened and how it got to that point. I felt like a bad mother to my children. I thought about becoming what Robert was, a cheater, and I didn't want to be a hypocrite. I even had the crazy notion that if I were to stay home long enough that John would forget about the kiss. Of course, that wasn't going to happen. Eventually, I had to deal with it, so I went back to work and the first face I saw was John. He was waiting outside for me to pull up in the parking lot. He came over to my car and opened my door and asked if I was all right. I told him that I was okay, but I thought that we needed to talk about what happened. He agreed, but we never did. We continued on day to day, but we ended up cutting our lunches to few and far in between.

Meanwhile, back on the home front, Robert asked if I wanted to go shoot pool with him. I remember thinking; "Oh boy, he knows what I did." I may as well deal with it now and get it over with. After settling the girls' at my mother's for the evening, we went out and actually enjoyed ourselves until Robert had too much to drink. It seemed as if I would irk him if I breathed too loud. Alcohol really took over his brain cells. We ended up leaving the pool hall early and I asked Robert what was the problem and he just kept on about Dana, at which point, I found out that he had just left her home in a rage over a fight they had. He was beating her as well.

25

While still angry about Dana, he decided to take it out on me and he pulled over behind huge buildings where there were no street lights and threw me a blow on the left side of my jaw. The right side of my head hit my window *(I still have a knot on the right side of my forehead to this day)* and as I put my face in my hands, he was already out of the car, came to my side, opened the door, drug me out and pulled off.

I was devastated. I didn't know what to do. I proceeded to walk home after hiding in the bushes of a McDonald's for about an hour crying. I didn't want to be seen on the streets bleeding. It must have been past 3 o'clock in the morning. When I got in the door, he was passed out on the couch snoring. I tried to come in the door quietly for fear of him waking up and trying to have his way with me as he always did after he beat on me. I called it rape. Unfortunately, I wasn't quiet enough. I tripped in the doorway, not having clear vision because of the tears and blood in my eyes, and the noise woke him up. He asked me where I'd been as if he didn't remember and I told him that I had to walk home because he hit me and left me and he apologized and promised, as usual, that he would never put his hands on me again after looking at the left side of my jaw being swollen from his blow and the blood trickling down the right side of my forehead. I knew better and I knew what came next. He began having his way with me again. When he was finished doing his business, he fell asleep on top of me. I tried sliding out from underneath him and he woke up enough to move down to the floor from the couch and I ran upstairs to jump in the shower and scrubbed myself raw. I scrubbed so much that I was sore and it would burn like hell whenever I had to urinate. It was the weekend, but I still had to work from 3 P.M.-11 P.M. that next day. I couldn't wait to get to work so I could get away from him. A few hours into my shift, I paged John with a voice mail message and told him that I was working tonight and that I needed to talk to him. He showed up 30 minutes after I left him the message and sat with me all that day and night until my shift was over. John was angry after looking at my bruises, but there wasn't much he could do, except for what he already doing...was being my friend.

A year had passed and the situation between Robert and I had attempted to improve. He finally stopped seeing Dana, but his family was still in our business. I guess I couldn't have everything my way. The friendship between John and I was still going strong. We continued to tell each other of our problems at home, but shortly after, my problems began to cease. Robert had stopped drinking cold turkey; he stopped beating on me, and started asking to make love to me. He was becoming the Robert I met 11 ½ years ago.

Beginning to finally enjoy my home life and marriage after being out of love with Robert for over 2 ½ years, I started to fall in love with him all over again. I would tell Robert I loved him 3 or 4 times a day, every single day. I felt that this was a new beginning for us. We even started going to church every Sunday. It was beautiful. Robert, our girls, and even I got baptized. At that point in my life, I wanted to be completely right for my "new husband," so I cut the ties of my friendship with John. I had to because our attraction for one another was too strong, it just wasn't right. John didn't take it too well and even shed quite a few tears. He told me that he loved me and that it wasn't fair. Feeling badly about the situation, I began to shed a few tears myself, but this was something that had to be done. I appreciated John and his friendship; however, we had to put an end to it before we allowed ourselves to go beyond our friendship, which was so easy to do because John and I loved each other. (*I will always love John and he will always be embedded in my soul of wonderful memories.*)

I removed myself from the situation and resigned with the hospital for the last time and went back to rebuilding my business and clientele. For some reason, it seemed so much easier than the first time a few years back. Business was going so well that I ended up with a clientele of 15 that included two major hospitals, several physicians' offices throughout cities in Virginia, a medical center in California, and a few law firms, with a staff of 12 to perform the work. Robert was encouraging and very supportive. What started out as $50-$75 per week grew from $48,000 to $75,000 over a three year period. Life couldn't be sweeter.

His family members didn't have too much to say anymore, but they still wouldn't give me my props. Jealousy played a big role within them, especially in Victoria. She was so obvious, but I turned her negative attitude towards me into a positive and thought that there must be something wonderful about me that she just can't keep my name out of her mouth. My attitude towards her ignorance only made her angrier and she didn't come around as much because she didn't like what she saw…me, whom she despised, making it on my own merit from a business I built from nothing.

Eventually, we moved from a 3 bedroom, 2 bath single family townhouse to a 4 bedroom, 3 bathroom home in an upscale neighborhood of Virginia Beach. We had two SUVs and a Mustang convertible. The girls' schools were directly on the corner, so we could stand on our front porch and see the entire school at the corner of our street. It was a beautiful arrangement, with me working from home. Robert decided that since I took care of his father that he wanted to help take care of my mother, and the girls were very close to her, so he thought it would be a great idea if she moved in with us. He begged and begged Mother to give up her apartment.

Finally, after many, many attempts and a few months in between of asking, my mother said yes. He made a deal with her that we would pay most of the rent of $1150 per month and all the utilities. She only had to pay $475.00 and take care of her car payment and her phone bill. It all sounded good to me. I thought to myself that Robert had finally grown up. With mother's job being less than 5 minutes away from our new home, this move was very convenient for her. For the first year in our home, we had a ball. We had already made plans to purchase the house after the second year. During the week, it was such a hassle for everyone with work and school for the girls that I kept a home cooked meal for everyone when they came home. Sometimes Robert and I would meet up for lunch. My husband had his clothes ironed and ready for the week and I would run his bath water after we ate dinner together.

It was like a dream, but it was very much real. On Saturday mornings, we would all pile into one of the SUVs to show mother other parts of Virginia and be gone all day 'til dark. Every Sunday after church, we would come home and smell breakfast, compliments of mother. She would make us lunch and dinner as well on the weekends. Sunday evenings were our family bingo nights. Mother would have already gone to the department store and purchased gift items for the bingo winners. We were all happy, or so I thought. I continued to tell Robert how much I loved him and I guess it was too much for him, because right after I would tell him, he would say, "Didn't you just say that?" He would say it in a way that my "I love you's" were irritating him. That's when the enemy found a way to creep back into our home.

Shortly afterwards, Robert's sister-in-law, Kayla, who was married to his brother, Malcolm, who just so happened to be mother's supervisor. Before the fluctuation of my company and our big move, mother and Kayla got along great. Then after our blessings came about, Kayla got a whiff of how well my company was doing and where we were residing. All this came from Victoria. Kayla and Victoria were close and were good company for each other by being miserable and jealous. Victoria began coming around with her phony way of pretending she actually liked me just to get more gossip to take to Kayla. This wasn't good at all. I could smell the evil reeking off her. Soon after, Robert stopped wanting to go to church and Kayla began treating my mother like total shit. She started writing mother up for petty things that weren't even infractions just to try and get her fired. My mother was trying to hang on so she could get her 10 years in for retirement, from which she was only a few months away. It took a toll on my mother. She would come home from work and go straight to her room, shut her door, and not even come down for dinner. I would take her a plate to make sure she ate and she would proceed to telling me how her days had been going with Kayla being on her back. I felt helpless and angry at the same time. My first instinct was to go pay Kayla a visit, but that would have only made things worse for mother so I confided in Robert. He pretended to care, but it was apparent that he didn't.

27

He soon began to slip back into his old ways minus the physical abuse and alcohol, but continued with the mental abuse. He started hanging out again. When the negativity took place, Victoria disappeared. I looked at it as if "Her work here was done."

Robert's hanging out got to the point of him not coming home until it was time for him to go to work the next day. Hang up phone calls would start again and I assumed it was Dana, but it wasn't. This was somebody new. One day, my business phone rang and the voice on the other end was a man that said his name was Mike. He proceeded to tell me what my husband's name was and my name and where we lived and where he worked. He said that he and my husband had a mutual friend, but he didn't give her name and told me that she and my husband were having an affair. My heart just dropped and I was speechless. I just listened quietly on the other end, trying not to cry. Here we were after making so much progress; now we were back to square one. Mike said that he had spoken to my husband on several occasions to leave the girl alone and reminded him that he was married, but Robert's response was, "that he didn't care." Mike ended the phone call by telling me how sorry he was, but he felt that I needed to know. At least now, I knew where all the phone hang-ups were coming from. I knew it was all too good to be true. I knew it was coming eventually, but I wasn't prepared for what came next.

I confronted Robert about what I was informed of and he didn't deny anything, he just tried to turn it around and say that it was all in my head, and then in the same breath, stated that someone was playing a game with me. I told him the gentleman's name and the details he knew and Robert had an answer for that, saying that he talks to people every day or it could have been an enemy from his present job, but I knew he was lying. Why would the person call on my business phone instead of the home phone? I believed Mike and had no other indications that he was lying to me. I asked Robert where he was when he didn't come home and he flipped and walked out. I didn't see him for a week. Wherever he was, he must have had work clothes there because he certainly didn't come home to get any. The kids would ask, "Where's Daddy?" I didn't know what to say except, "He'll be home soon." Deep down, I wished he would come home or even call, but he didn't. By this time, Mother knew what was going on and thought it would be a good idea if she left. She had already made arrangements for my brothers to come down to move her back home. I wholeheartedly understood, but I just couldn't follow. I didn't know what I wanted to do at this point, but I knew that I didn't want to leave my business or my home.

A week had gone by and Robert came home, but only to pack his clothes. It was our middle child's 10th birthday and I tried not to appear so upset in order to make her birthday a happy one, but it didn't turn out that way. The girls were downstairs in the kitchen waiting for us to come down to sing "Happy Birthday" to her, but all they heard were my cries and his yelling. I found myself on my knees, begging Robert to stay and continuously asking him why was he doing this and he just kept telling me that I was crazy and he had to go. I held onto his ankles as he was dragging me along out of the bedroom into the hallway. I let go when he got to the steps. He came back upstairs to gather the rest of his clothing and when he was all packed up, he told me that he didn't love me anymore and took off his wedding rings and placed them in the Bible. He said that he was angry with me for wanting to move to Virginia before his parents died. I didn't understand where that was coming from since his father spent his last dying moments with me taking care of him. Then he changed it and said that it was my mother, but he was the one that begged her to come live with us. I just took them for what they were…excuses.

I later found out that Robert left us to be with another woman and her two children. I begged him to at least come and sing "Happy Birthday" before he left for good and he agreed to do so. By this time, Mother went up to her room to avoid seeing Robert. All three of the girls' eyes were full of tears, as were mine. I was so upset that I couldn't stop vomiting. Before I could speak, every third word was vomit in the kitchen sink.

28

Shortly afterwards, we sang "Happy Birthday" and Robert then walked out the door and abandoned us. Our daughter said that her birthday would never be the same again. She told me that all this time she thought that, "Daddy wasn't like all the other guys, but he really is." This hurt me to my heart and I could do nothing but hold her. The girls and I stood in the kitchen, holding each other, crying tears full of confusion and pain.

With all the reminiscing and traveling for more than 8 hours, the trip had taken its toll on me. I fell asleep at the wheel and ended up driving off the road. Savon was behind me and noticed what I had done and blew his horn a few times to alert me. We pulled over and sat for a few minutes so I could wake up. All that thinking about the past took me to another place, but it made me look forward to Georgia even more. Looking at the time and even with my little set back, we were still pretty much on schedule. We went back to our journey and after several hours passed we saw the big Peach and soon after, we saw Atlanta. We finally arrived. The girls were screaming with joy. Right away, I felt an overwhelming peace. I was here…my destination on a new road to a new life.

CHAPTER 7

Luke 11:8 - I tell you, even though he will not get up and give you the bread because of friendship, yet because of your shameless audacity, he will surely get up and give you as much as you need.

We were entering into the onslaught of traffic that Atlanta has. It was outrageous, but for some reason, I didn't seem to mind it at all. I was just looking around at all the people smiling. I bet they thought I was crazy or something, but I was so happy. We were approximately 45 minutes away from our new apartment in Marietta. We were checking out the sites as we journeyed to our destination in the extreme heat that Atlanta has. We were sweaty, smelly, and hungry, but we didn't want to stop until we got to the apartment. Finally, we found it - Chimney Hill Apartments off Windy Hill Road. It was so nice. It was no way near the home we left in Virginia, but there was something different about this apartment...it was ours, and just ours, a new start.

The girls and I had this tradition of whenever we got a new place; we would roll ourselves across the floor in every room. This was our way of christening our home. We were all smiles. We didn't unload the truck right away. Instead we drove to the nearest chicken place to get something to eat and found Popeye's Chicken just down the street. We took it back to the apartment and ate and talked about how long it took us to get to Georgia. Being that I already had the utilities and phone turned on a week before we moved, I brung the phone in from my vehicle to make sure it was on. I plugged it up and got a dial tone. The first person on my list to call was Mother. She was so glad that we made it safely and said that she would call me later tonight to make sure we were settled in comfortably.

I then called Janet and left a message on her answering machine to let her know that we made it and left my number for her to call me back. Then the one person I couldn't wait to call was Karl. I had to remove myself from everyone in order to talk to him. I needed my privacy. I went into my bedroom and called Karl at the barracks and he picked it up on the first ring. He was waiting in his room for me to call he stated. He asked me how the girls liked their new home. I told him about our christening habit and he just laughed. He said he could tell how happy I was by the tone of my voice. A big difference from when we were in Virginia. I told Karl that I wanted to find a church immediately so he gave me his mother's phone number. He said that he had already told her about the girls and me. I thanked Karl for being such a wonderful friend and a big help. He said that it was a pleasure and that he was going to get something to eat and would call me later that evening. After unloading the truck for a few hours, I decided to take a breather and call Mrs. Grier. When she answered, I could remember thinking, she sounds like a nice woman, but I couldn't help the vibe I was getting, but I chose to ignore it and go with the flow. I introduced myself and told her that Karl gave me the number because I wanted information on a good church to attend. She commenced to telling me about the church she belonged to and how great her pastor was, so I decided to give it a try. I agreed to meet with her that following Sunday and we described ourselves so that we would recognize each other. As Savon finished up the last of the unloading of the truck, he stated that he had to leave right then and there to get back up home before it got too late. I expressed to my brother how grateful I was to him for moving me to Georgia. He really looked out for me. The kids and I gave him a hug and thanked him. We watched him pull off and I felt like I was really on my own now with no family in town and no more abuse from my soon-to-be ex-husband. I felt wonderful. I popped the cork on my bottle of wine and drank me a glass after five years of not drinking and felt wonderful. My spirit felt free.

As it was getting later and later, the girls started getting sleepier and sleepier, so we put their beds together and pulled clean sheets out of the laundry basket and made their beds up so they could sleep comfortably. I stayed up half the night unpacking boxes, putting things together, and hanging up pictures. I was always known to unpack a home in one night, no matter where we moved. I just wanted to feel lived in and comfortable when I got up the next morning. I got a break that night when Karl called me back. He asked me if I had a chance to call his mother. I told him that we made arrangements to meet at church the following Sunday. I told him what I was attempting to do with unpacking the whole apartment and trying to get everything set up and he just laughed. He thought that I should try to get some sleep, but I was too pumped and excited to do that. I had already finished the bedrooms, except for a few things, like unpacking the clothes.

After taking a break for a few hours of talking with Karl, we finally said our good nights. However, I still wasn't tired from being so excited about being in Georgia in my own apartment, and so I began to finish up the unpacking. I didn't lie down to rest until I actually saw daylight. The girls came into my room and asked if I pulled another one of my usual routines and I informed them that I had. As understanding as they are, they shut my door and finished unpacking the clothes that I neglected. I must have slept all that morning into the late afternoon.

Chapter *8*

Esther 8:16 - For the Jews it was a time of happiness and joy, gladness and honor.

A few days went by and we were enjoying our new home and new environment. We went for a test drive in an attempt to find the church that we were going to meet Mrs. Grier at. On the way there, we got lost and ended up in an unpleasant part of town. There was no one around to ask directions of except a group of brothas hanging out on the street corner, looking intimidating as hell. At first, I was skeptical to ask them for anything, but they were the only ones around. I pulled over and asked them if they could help me and right away they swarmed to the car and said, "Sure baby, whatever you need." So I told them that I was looking for a church and the name of the street the church was on and their whole personas changed. They looked in the car and noticed the girls and they became gentlemen. They started asking each other if they knew of the church and luckily, a few of them did. I thanked them and they smiled and told me to take care. They gave me great directions which took us right to the church with no problem. The girls asked, "Mommy, weren't you scared to talk to them?" and I told them that I was at first, but we shouldn't be afraid of people, no matter what they look like. I reminded them never to judge a book by its cover. Sometimes the hellish looking people can be the sweetest and the sweetest looking ones can be devils.

Sunday approached and it was time to try out a new church and to meet Karl's mother. I was so nervous and tried not to appear anxious. Overall, I was more curious as to what she looked liked, if Karl got his looks from his mother or from his father. As we were entering the church, I caught glimpses of every woman and was comparing them to Karl, trying to peep out his mother before she could peep me out. We sat through the entire service, but didn't meet Mrs. Grier until the end. She came up to me and introduced herself. She said that I was the only woman there with three little girls so she knew right away who we were. Mrs. Grier was a petit woman, light complexion, about 5' tall, with a strong southern accent. Karl looked just like her. Same eyes, mouth, and cheekbones. We agreed to eat breakfast at a McDonald's down the street from the church. She complimented me on how nice looking my girls were and then asked the question of what brought me to Georgia. I don't know what made me say this, but the stupid words that came out of my mouth were "Karl." Why did I voice that out loud? The last thing I wanted was for her to think that I was chasing after her son. Her mouth dropped and she had a surprised look on her face and I quickly proceeded to explain my stupid ass comment with, "Karl told me about the schools and colleges here as far as the girls' were concerned, and how nice of a state it is to raise children in."

As I was explaining myself, the look on her face changed for the better and I could tell that she understood where I was coming from. I then told her about my going through a divorce, but not too much detail of what led up to it. As our conversation continued on about life, church, and God, the more comfortable I felt with her. The girls' were so comfortable and being as friendly as they are by nature, they asked her to come over to our apartment after breakfast and to my surprise, she agreed. I was shocked, but I couldn't have that look on my face in front of her, so I said, "Let's go." She followed us to our apartment and the whole time en route I remember thinking, "I can't believe Karl's mother is coming to my home." I drilled the girls about their behavior and about when talking to her to say "Yes, ma'am" and "No, ma'am." When we arrived, I offered Mrs. Grier something to drink and asked her if I could get her anything besides that to try to make her feel at home, but she said she was quite comfortable. I could tell she was comfortable with us because she kicked off her shoes, lit a cigarette, and laid back. I was glad that she felt the way she did in my presence. I excused the girls and myself and we changed out of our church clothes into some casual outfits. I told Mrs. Grier to feel free to walk herself through our humble abode and to help herself to anything in the refrigerator. After viewing our home, the girls brought out our photo album to show Mrs. Grier.

Our family album was always our way of letting you know that we liked you. I had hoped she didn't notice Robert's pictures missing because the girls wanted to cut out his pictures from all our photos. I looked at it as a healing process for them. Afterwards, the girls went to the neighborhood playground and Mrs. Grier and I sat out on the balcony to get to know each other more. She didn't hesitate to ask me about Robert and what led up to us getting a divorce. I proceeded to tell her about how he left us for another woman and her children and how we were here in Georgia to get a new lease on life. She proceeded to tell me about personal things involving Mr. Grier and about how they weren't getting along. The whole entire time I was talking with her, I just couldn't believe that this was Karl's mother. She felt like an old friend and we were just venting about our lives. We were comfortable with each other and it went beyond having Karl in common. It had nothing to do with Karl at all. We talked about everything, down to current events and our children. We spoke about our children like two women with children do, regarding the silly and funny things they sometimes say and do. She spoke about Karl as if she was talking to a woman of her age. I was three years older than Karl and Mrs. Grier was about 14 years older than me. I never had a problem communicating with anyone older than myself. I was always told that I had an old soul. The way she spoke about Karl was as if he was a young child instead of a grown man, as I saw him, but the more she talked about him and his brother in this certain way she had, I felt like I was her age and I had a crush on her young son. It didn't feel the same. My feelings towards Karl were genuine and true. I really liked Karl and he and I shared the same views about parenting and we got along so well, but she made me feel like a dirty old woman lusting after a young man. I didn't know if that was her game plan or what, but she succeeded on that front.

The time flew by quickly. I asked her if she wanted to stay for dinner, but she declined; however, she asked us over to her home for breakfast the following Sunday after church. I thought to myself, "Wow, this is great." Of course, I took her up on the offer. During that week, the girls were getting settled into their new schools and I was trying to get back on track with my business and my new job. It was working out perfectly. Here I was, dealing with a man's mother, whom I liked and actually felt that the feeling was mutual with, unlike Robert's mother. After dealing with Robert's mother, I judged every man's mother a bit harshly, but it wasn't like that at all this time.

Robert's mother took ignorance to a whole other level. After 15 years of dealing with his side of the family, here I was about to turn the page of a new book and actually live a normal life with a man I adored and his mother, who actually talked to me like I was a human being. Saturday rolled around and Karl and I were talking about the meeting with his mother and the date for breakfast on Sunday. I told him that I liked his mother very much and how comfortable I felt with her. Karl was in disbelief that she actually came to my home and how long she stayed for. He was too ecstatic about the whole thing. I didn't know what to think about that, but for some reason I got a funny vibe that I couldn't dismiss at first, but I found a way to do so. Karl and I talked about the girls and he asked how they were adjusting to the big change in their lives and I told him that from what I was observing in their behavior, they were getting along great. They loved that they were somewhere that no one knew them and they were looking forward to making new friends. What I liked about Karl the most was the fact that he didn't seem to care how many children I had and what my situation was. He said that he once went with a young lady for five years that had five children. He said that he loved kids. Every time we spoke either by phone or e-mail, he would start the conversation off with, "How are the girls doing?" He would proceed with asking if we ate and what we ate. His caring and sincerity made me melt.

That Sunday morning, I got a call from Mrs. Grier, stating to bring a change of clothes with us so we can switch into some casual clothes instead of being in our Sunday best all day. The first thing that came to mind was how this was all too good to be true. Could it be this easy, with meeting someone and being accepted by a family so quickly? I had never experienced anything like that before, so of course, I was a bit skeptical about it all, but it didn't stop me from going with the flow.

The whole time, that same feeling of "Something just isn't right" continued to linger over my head, but I kept it in the background, trying to dismiss it. When we arrived at church, Mrs. Grier held a seat for us to sit with her during service. She mentioned that her son dropped her off and that she would ride with us to her home afterwards. Quite naturally, I assumed she was speaking of her younger son, Karl's brother Mark, so I didn't think anything of it. I was excited to meet him as well.

Mrs. Grier struck me to be a nice woman, but there was something about her that I couldn't quite put my finger on. It set off a strange vibe within me. I couldn't call it, but that vibe was so strong that I didn't want to dismiss it either. After service, we piled up in my Explorer and Mrs. Grier directed us to her home. She didn't live far from the church. When we pulled up into her driveway, I noticed a nice home in a residential neighborhood that was quiet and full of black folks with large homes and nice cars in the driveway. It was so nice to see. She said Karl should be back in a few minutes and I thought to myself, "Did I hear her right, did she say Karl?" I had just spoken to Karl the night before and that week before and he never mentioned that he was going to be in town. What exactly was the deal here and why didn't he tell me? I thought it was strange and my vibe remained. We went in and she gave us a tour of her home, which was decent. It looked very much lived in. Comfortable. She told us to go and change into our casual clothes while she got breakfast started. The girls and I went to her downstairs den/TV room area where there was a bathroom and we all changed together. I asked the girls if they were okay and they were too excited about being there and commented on how nice Mrs. Grier seemed to be. They were really enjoying themselves. I was glad that they were happy. After we finished changing, we went upstairs to offer help, but she said she was just fine. So we sat upstairs anyway to keep her company and just then the doorbell rang. She said that it was Karl. She went to answer and there he was. Just as fine as the day we met. My heart was all a flutter. He came into the kitchen where the girls and I were sitting and spoke to everyone. My nerves were getting bad and the vibe was getting stronger. I didn't know what to think. I just didn't understand why no one said anything to me about Karl being in town.

The girls and I set the table and Karl helped his mother in the kitchen with lying the breakfast out on the table like a buffet. Everything smelled and looked so good. I wanted to dig right on in, but I was trying to be cute with Karl in my presence, so I ate like a bird, especially with him sitting directly across the table from me. I caught his eye a few times staring at me and when I did, Mrs. Grier didn't miss a beat with having her eyes on me as well, but it looked as if I was catching glimpses at Karl instead of the way it really was. That didn't set right with me because she didn't look at me with admiration; she looked at me as if I was looking at her man. It was strange.

CHAPTER *9*

Job 6:20 - They are distressed, because they had been confident; they arrive there, only to be disappointed.

After break.ast, we all got into my Explorer and took the girls to the neighborhood park. Karl stood up against the wall while Mrs. Grier and I sat on the bench and the girls just explored the park swings, monkey bars, etc. We were talking about everyday things, like current events, when one of the neighborhood children that Mrs. Grier knew fell down and she proceeded to walk over towards the child. When she did, Karl started walking towards me to sit in her spot and he asked his mother if she was coming back. When she noticed that Karl was about to sit down next to me, she couldn't get back to the bench quick enough. She told the kid that fell, "You'll be all right" and she walked away and gave Karl a look as if to say, "You know better." I didn't understand the whole incident and I couldn't believe what I had just seen. I thought to myself "Did that just happen?" There was something definitely not right about the whole thing. Was he not allowed to sit beside me, or even talk to me for that matter, because he certainly was quiet at breakfast (except to answer the girls when they talked to him and to answer his mother). My heart was beginning to ache because it made me feel like my presence wasn't really welcomed. We were just invited because she was welcomed into our home and she wanted to return the favor. I was beginning to feel uncomfortable. I wanted so badly to just go home, but the girls were having a great time. When she came back to the bench, she asked me about Robert. I told her what the deal was with him and that our divorce was soon to be final and she asked about how the girls felt. I told her that they were angry with him because of him leaving and the reasons behind that, which was understandable. However, her questions weren't out of concern, it seemed like she wanted me to feel hurt and actually show it. She kept drilling me with, "I know you got to still love him and have feelings for him and want him back." I thought to myself, "Where are you going with this, woman?", but I was nice in my reply of, "He left me, so why want someone that obviously doesn't want you?" I told her that it didn't matter how long we were together, I was much stronger than that. I wasn't a weak woman with low self- esteem. I was and am very much aware of how beautiful I am on the inside as well as the outside. She just didn't know me very well. She even went as far as to say she didn't believe me and that she would tell me when I was over him. Huh...did she really say that? What in the hell did she mean she would tell me when I was over Robert? Who in the hell did she think she was? I wasn't one of her boys, who she told how to feel things and when to feel them. My own mother wouldn't dare tell me anything like that. I didn't understand her and suddenly, she looked more like interference instead of a friend.

She went on to tell me about Mr. Grier and how his infidelities were taking a heavy toll on their marriage and how it made her feel. At that moment, I felt she was comparing my past with her present, but we were in totally different situations. I was away from Robert; she was still with her husband and going through changes with him. I saw her as a bitter, unhappy woman and though misery loves company, I wasn't going to allow her to put me in the same boat as her. Every time she said something negative, I would come back with something positive. Our back and forth conversation was interrupted by my youngest daughter walking up to Karl and asking him to give her a push on the swing. Of course, Mrs. Grier was about-faced at that situation. Karl was so happy to do it that he even picked her up to take her to the swing, until he caught his mother's eye and then he immediately put her down. I was really tripping over how this woman was really tripping and how Karl was looking more and more to me like a "mama's boy" instead of a man. She ran him from top to bottom. It was obvious she had total control over him anytime; all she had to do was give him a look. In their presence was not where I wanted to be at that moment. I was so ready to go. I told my oldest daughter to let the other two know that we were getting ready to go home.

I remembered in speaking with Karl at the beginning of him telling me that he told his mother about everything that went on in his life, at which time a red flag went up with me right there. I just wondered what he told her about me, if anything. He couldn't have said anything negative because I know that I never presented myself in a negative way towards him - otherwise, he would not have kept in contact with me for three months. It was just mind boggling and I didn't want to deal with that type of unnecessary drama. My girls came over to me and asked if I was ready and I told them yes, that I didn't want to wear out our welcome with our visit and Mrs. Grier intervened with "Don't go yet, we'll just go back to the house and watch television" and that the girls weren't ready to go home yet. Of course, she knew what to say in the presence of children because my girls ate that up and asked if they could stay with these big smiles on their faces. I didn't want to say no and look like a mean mommy, so I agreed for their sake. The girls were really enjoying themselves. We went back to her home and we all settled downstairs and watched television.

Later in the afternoon, Mrs. Grier made the girls some ice cream. Karl sat next to me on the couch and I asked him why he didn't call me to tell me that he was going to be in town. He replied with, "I wanted to, but she kept having me go here and there, picking up stuff. Now I knew that Karl was three years younger than I was, and that really wasn't much of an age difference. However, I didn't know that his mind was so damn young. He seemed like a totally different person in his mother's presence from when we talked on the phone. I was so disappointed. As time passed on and the girls were getting sleepy, I told Mrs. Grier that I thought it was a good idea that we get home before it got too late and that we had to get ready for the next week of work and school. She and Karl walked us out to our vehicle. The girls gave them both a hug and we thanked her for everything, but I only hugged her. I wouldn't dare hug Karl in front of her. Who knows what she would have done? She probably would have jumped in between us. Karl kept staring at me nonstop and must have realized that he was staring in front of his mother and quickly looked at her and walked away. I was like; did that actually happen just now? It was crazy as hell. Then their phone rang and Karl answered it and thank goodness it was for his mother. She went inside to take her call and Karl came back out into the driveway with me and I asked him to call me later. He just looked at me as if I hadn't said anything at all. The look on his face was like, he wanted to tell me something, but he couldn't. Then he uttered that he would come by before he caught a flight back to the barracks in Florida. Something told me to not believe that. Just then Mrs. Grier came back out on a cordless phone. I guess to make sure nothing was exchanged between Karl and I like hugs or kisses. This was ridiculous. I couldn't wait to get home.

A week had passed by and I hadn't heard a thing from Karl, so I decided to call him. I left several messages at his job and at his room in the barracks, but no return calls. I didn't know what to think. Later on the next evening, he called. He said that he had to go out to sea. This put up so many red flags it wasn't even funny because I had just seen his mother in church Sunday and she asked me if Karl called me because he called her to tell her about his week at work. I didn't mention anything about what his mother told me. I just continued on with the conversation and asked him what was going with him and why he had been so distant at his mother's home and why he was acting like he really didn't want to talk to me at the moment. To avoid answering my questions he said that he had to go and that he would call me later, but later got to be never.

Every Sunday we would sit with Mrs. Grier and she would always ask me if Karl called me. Of course I would tell her no and that seemed like it put a smile on her face. I didn't know what to make out of the whole ordeal, so I decided to remove myself from being in her presence so much. I missed a few Sunday services and decided to find another church. I told the girls that I didn't think it was a good idea to stay in contact with her because she didn't seem right to me. My girls and I are so close and they always trust my judgment, so they said it was fine with them and they didn't like my facial expressions whenever I was in Mrs. Grier's presence so
they agreed that it would be a good idea as well.

After not hearing from me for close to a month, Mrs. Grier called and asked if everything was all right with the girls and myself because she hadn't seen us in church in a while. I told her that everything was all right, but I thought that the church was too far out for us to come every Sunday and that I was going to find another one closer to our area since the church was in deep Atlanta and we lived in Marietta. I knew that she wasn't going to hang up that phone without asking me if I heard from Karl and I told her that I hadn't and she commenced to telling me that she told Karl that she felt I was too mature for him and he was too immature to be with me and that he was too young to handle my situation. She stated that part as if I had major problems. I thought to myself, how dare she say such a thing to him. But his dumb ass listened to her instead of doing what he felt. So that was the deal with him acting strange in front of her and her looks towards him. I was furious, but I didn't let on. I didn't really have much to say to her after that. She left me speechless. I tried to get off the subject and told her that the girls and I were on our way out the door to go to the store. It was a lie, but I wanted her to get off the phone because I didn't want to be disrespectful to her by expressing my anger.

After I hung up the phone, I told myself that she or Karl would not hear from me again. So this was life after marriage and children. I knew it was going to get worse before it got better. My vibes were right about her all along. From now on, I was not going to dismiss my instincts. I was really hurt and disappointed by Karl. He had me fooled. I thought he was a real man. He certainly put on a big front. What happened to the words he spoke to me? He seemed so sincere and I actually believed he was, up until the point when he let his mother know. The many phone calls he used to give me just ceased. It was all strange to me because Karl was 26 years old. Maybe he was too young mentally. He certainly showed me he wasn't a man to just distance himself like he did based on his mother's negative words to him. I just didn't understand how you could feel something for someone, express yourself to them in all aspects, and then, at the drop of a mother's words, just be gone like that. I will never understand that and I was tired of trying. I just gave up on the whole thing and kept my focus on my girls and my career.

CHAPTER *10*

Matthew 7:15 - "Watch out for false prophets. They come to you in sheep's clothing, but inwardly they are ferocious wolves.

As time passed, the girls and I were adjusting to Georgia, our new apartment, their school, and my career just fine. It was smooth sailing until the job that got us to Georgia went bankrupt. The whole damn company turned belly up and everyone, including supervisors, managers, etc. was out of a job. This mishap was certainly not anything I needed at this point in time. My car note was due and so was rent. This wasn't cool at all. Then to top it off, I wasn't getting any kind of child support. I had no other choice but to call Robert and ask for help. Not having the number to where he was living with his new girlfriend, I paged him with my number instead. I waited patiently, with my heart feeling like it was about to beat out of my chest. I was scared and nervous as to how he was going to react. It was hard to tell because he had so many faces and I surely didn't want any drama, not at this moment in my life. The phone rang and I answered with a quiver in my voice. Robert didn't sound upset or rude; he sounded as if he was glad to hear from me. He proceeded to tell me what a mistake he had made by leaving us and how much hell his girlfriend was putting him through. I thought to myself, why in the hell is he talking to me like this, telling me about a girl he left me for? He was a little too comfortable. I interrupted him with the situation we were in and asked him for child support. It didn't take long for his other face to appear. Robert started out with saying, "No one told you to move my kids down there and have them living in poverty," and then he changed up quickly and was quiet for a moment and asked how much did I need. I told him that my last paycheck should cover the rent, but I needed help with the car note. He assured me that it wasn't a problem and that he would send me a check right away, which he did.

Shortly afterwards, Robert continued to call. He would ask about the girls, but would never want to speak to them, even when I told him that they were right beside me. I guess he felt ashamed, which he should have. Every time Robert called, he would say negative things about Felicia, the girl he left us for. He would tell me how he caught her in so many lies about her age (she told him that she was 29 and she was actually 35 per her driver's license). Then she told him that she used to work in a mental ward when actually, she had been a patient. It really started to bother Robert because he would call me around 2 or 3 o'clock in the morning. I would listen to him because knowing that he was beginning to pay for his abandonment was pleasure enough for me. Janet called me a few days later and asked how we were doing in Georgia. I told her what happened with the job and that I had to call Robert. I also told her about Robert's new drama and she was kind of upset with me for even giving him the time of day listening to him. I told her that it was a personal pleasure of mine, but she still disagreed. She thought it was strange. I guess it is, but it was a part of my healing process. I didn't expect her or anyone else to understand.

While on my search for another job, I went to a hospital in Atlanta, close to Decatur, and applied for a job. While on my mission, I spotted this handsome brotha with the look of Genuine (the singer) and the body of a linebacker. His name was Jesse. Jesse had these pearly white teeth, all straight, and all his. Beautiful smile, handsome face. This brotha really had it going on. He had the look, the size, a nice height of 6' 0". He was all of that. Jesse worked in the business office of the hospital and approached me and asked if there was anything he could do for me. Homeboy just didn't know. I told him that I was looking for human resources so I could drop off my resume. He said that he would walk me there if I didn't mind. My first thought was, I hope I don't slip and fall in these new high heel shoes. I hope I don't have any lipstick on my teeth. I hope my appearance is on point. He asked me my name and what kind of job was I looking for.

I told him everything he wanted to know about me, my children, and that we were new to Atlanta. He was a 25-year-old semi-newcomer to Atlanta hailing from Richmond, Virginia. He actually moved to Georgia about five months before we did. He stated that he and I could hang because he simply wasn't "feeling" the Georgia girls. He asked if he could call me sometime and the first thing that came to my mind were my girls, so I told him that I would take his number instead of giving out mine.

After getting to human resources, filling out an application, and dropping off my resume, Jesse actually waited until I was done and walked me to my car. He said to have a nice day and wished me luck with getting the job. In the meantime, not stopping at just one, I had already applied for several more jobs and one came through. I started the job in the same field as my "on hold" business to keep my skills intact. It was all good because I still had the opportunity to work from home.

Feeling good about getting a job so quickly, the girls and I celebrated with a bowl of popcorn, cookies, potato chips, and punch. We danced around the apartment listening to V-103, one of the great radio stations in Georgia. All the dancing and eating that we did pooped the girls out, but I was too excited to sleep. I thought about Jesse and decided to give him a call. When he answered I asked him if he remembered who I was and he said of course, and commenced to asking me if the hospital called me yet in regards to my application and resume. I told him no, but that another job came through. He said he would like to take me out to celebrate if I didn't mind, so I thought, why not, the girls are already settled, so we agreed to meet at a halfway point.

I told the girls that I was going to go out for a bit and I left my pager number and cell phone if they needed me, but they said they were fine and to go and enjoy myself. The girls always so understood and they never had a problem with being home alone whenever Robert and I would go out for the evening. They always did real well. They were so mature at 12, 10, and 6. My 12- year-old was more like 20 and the 10-year-old was more like 25. My 6-year-old was more like out of this world. She ran the other two. After freshening up a bit, I set out to meet Jesse. We decided to meet at a sports bar in Decatur. Pulling up, he was in the parking lot waiting for me.

After I parked, Jesse walked towards my car and politely opened my door and gave me a hug. When we got inside, he ordered us a Corona beer with a twist of lemon and paid for a pool table so I could show him my skills. Now, I hadn't had a drink of anything in over five years, except for my bottle of "new apartment wine" when we first moved to Georgia.

As the evening started playing out and we began having a good time with laughter and playing pool, I decided to call the girls and check on them. My 10-year-old answered and said that they were all right and was in bed. She asked if I was having a good time and I stated that I was. I told her that I would be home shortly. Jesse saw that I had just gotten off the phone and he asked if the girls were all right and I told him they were and were already settled in their beds. He stated to me how much he loved children. I didn't quite know where he was going with this, so I explained to him a little about my situation with Robert and that this dating thing was all new to me. He said that he understood and didn't want to rush me. He seemed sincere. As time was going on, I told him that I think I should get home. He asked if it was all right for him to have my number before we parted. I gave him my cell phone number instead. I thought he was decent. He damn sure was fine, but we know that looks aren't everything.

CHAPTER *11*

Isaiah 44:25 - who foils the signs of false prophets and makes fools of diviners, who overthrows the learning of the wise and turns it into nonsense

Four months went by and Jesse and I were getting along just great. We planned for an evening out and I informed the girls that he would be coming over to pick me up. I asked how they felt about it and they said that all they wanted was for me to be happy. As I was finishing up, Jesse rang the doorbell. I got nervous at the fact that I was having a man meet my daughters that wasn't their father. I opened the door and Jesse walked in and before I could introduce him, he started off with pointing them out and calling them by each other's name. This broke the ice real well with the girls. He got them to laugh. I excused myself to put on my lipstick and I heard them talking, telling Jesse what movie they were watching from Blockbuster Video. Jesse asked the girls what they liked to do for fun and they told him play games on their Play Station, but we couldn't get it to work because I didn't know how to hook it up. Well, Jesse certainly racked up some brownie points right away because he asked where it was and the girls took him right to the system and sure enough, he hooked the game up for them and instead of watching their Blockbuster movie, they played video games on their PlayStation.

As we were leaving, I reminded the girls that I would have my pager and cell phone on for them and without looking at me, they just waved me off. Jesse and I went out for a bite to eat at a local restaurant, and then afterwards we went on a drive around parts of Atlanta that I had never seen. It was so beautiful at night with all the lights.

I was so glad that I made the choice to come to Georgia. It just felt like home. As it was getting later, Jesse asked if I had any objections to going to his home with him and I assured him that I was fine with it. Besides, I wanted to see exactly how he was living and exactly where. We pulled up in the driveway of a quiet residential neighborhood of Decatur. He said that it was nice, but that he would be roommates with another gentleman in a few weeks. When I walked in, I noticed how clean it was. It was very well kept. We went into his bedroom and listened to some of his CD's. Jesse was an inspiring writer of raps. He shared his lyrics with me that he had written down in a notebook. He started reciting some of his rhymes to me and I thought to myself, this certainly is different. Is this what dating was? I didn't know. First, Jesse was five years younger than me. Second, I was used to my husband of 15 years that was five years older than me and Karl Grier didn't even count. I really didn't know what to expect, so I just went with the flow. The later it got, the sleepier I got. Jesse must have noticed my yawning that I didn't hide very well and asked if I was ready to go home. I told him that I had a wonderful time and that I was ready to go. On the way to my home, we talked about his moving and his roommate. His roommate was a 40-year-old truck driver named Albert. At first, it took me by surprise about their age difference and a red flag went up, but then I thought about how mature Jesse was, which dismissed my weird instincts and I let it go. After getting back to my home, Jesse walked me to my door and I asked him if he wanted to come in for a few minutes and he agreed. He sat on the couch and I went into the girls' bedroom to see if they were all right. The girls' were sound asleep. I went back out into the living room and sat on the couch next to Jesse and we watched a little television and talked about what was on and as I was watching him talk, I just leaned over and kissed him. With a surprising look on his face he asked me, "Where did that come from?" and I told him that "I wasn't sure, I just felt like doing it." He was such a gentleman with me throughout our four months of dating that I decided to make the first move. After kissing him, he leaned over, kissed me gently, started holding me tightly, and then suddenly, he stopped. Jesse apologized, excused himself, and said that it was time for him to leave. I didn't understand. I thought "Did my breath stink or maybe he didn't like the way I kissed?" I didn't know what it was, but another red flag came up.

I walked him to the door and reached out to embrace him and we kissed again. Jesse stated that he had to go and that it had nothing to do with me. He said that he wanted to remain a gentleman with me. I looked at him as being thoughtful and sincere. At this point in my life, I really wanted that from a man and he was right on time. I told him that I appreciated it, gave him a hug, and he said that he would call me. I didn't really expect to hear from him again. I was receiving a strange vibe from Jesse, but I couldn't quite put my finger on it. A few days had gone by and to my surprise he called to tell me that he and his roommate were moving into their new house. I asked him if I could be of assistance, but he said they had everything under control. It seemed like every two hours Jesse would call me. He said that he was letting me know that he was thinking about me. I thought about the other night with the intensity, then his all of a sudden stopping...I didn't know what to make of it. I never asked him about that night. I just enjoyed being spoiled with sincerity and the sweetness of his calling me the many times that he did in one night.

We made plans for Jesse to come over and have dinner with the girls and I. It was so nice. Our dinnertime was the best part of his visits. In between bites of our meals we were always laughing from the time dinner began until it was over. It would take a few hours for us to finish eating from laughing at Jesse so much. He was wonderful. The girls fell in love with him right away. I thought he would be "the one" for me. It didn't matter to me that he was five years younger than I. It was his personality that I enjoyed the most. Our dinnertime spent together soon became overnight stays. Jesse would bring an overnight bag and just go to work in the morning from my apartment. It felt like having a husband again. I would get up with the girls in the morning, see them off to school, then make Jesse's lunch and see him off to work.

My heart was happy. At lunchtime, he would call me to see how my day was going. Then he would call before he came to my apartment. He filled the gap that was missing in my life, but it all changed. It didn't take long for Jesse's true colors to show. He gave me this story of his car being in the shop and asked if he could use mine until his was taken care of. With Jesse needing my vehicle to go back and forth to work every day, this meant that he would have to stay with me during the week, which he did. Every time he came home, the more clothes he would bring. He had so many clothes that my dresser drawers were stuffed and I had to buy more hangers to put some in my closet. Then his shoes covered my closet floor. My bathroom now had a man's shaving kit and men's health and beauty aids. Jesse was practically living with us. I never asked any questions because I enjoyed his company and the girls were happy with him. He was a surrogate father to them. We were a family. However, when it came to bedtime, Jesse would never make a move. When he and I went to bed, we literally went to bed. There were no sexual relations between us. Even though we had been together for quite a while, I just thought he was being a gentleman or he didn't know how to approach me in that aspect because of our age difference.

However, when I made attempts, he would tell me that he was really tired and give me a peck on the forehead. I didn't want to force it, but I was beginning to have doubts. I confided in my sister Rolonda. When I told her of the changes in my household and all about Jesse, she wasn't too happy. She said that something wasn't right about him, but she would have to see his face or at least talk to him. She told me to get his belongings out of my home and to not allow him to drive my car anymore. Rolonda was a no biting her lip type of gal and she didn't take mess from anybody. If she knew anything, she knew men and how they operated. She asked me to describe Jesse a little more and when I did, she said with sternness in her voice, to get him out of there because he is stopping my blessings. She said that he was no good and a user. When I told her about us not having relations, but sleeping in the same bed together, she stated to me that he is either gay or has a woman. I trusted my sister and her judgment and took everything she told me into consideration. Instead of acting fast like she wanted me to, I wanted to see for myself what she saw in Jesse.

41

The weekend was here, but Jesse didn't come home and he didn't call. So I called the home he shared with his roommate Albert. Albert answered and said that Jesse told him that he wouldn't be home for the weekend. At that point, my heart dropped, but I didn't want to jump to any conclusions. Maybe Jesse was coming over later or would call me later, but he never did. The next time the phone rang, it was Albert. He asked me what I had planned for the evening and I told him nothing at all and that I was waiting for Jesse. Albert stated that he didn't think Jesse would be seen at all this weekend by either one of us.

Shortly afterwards, Albert and I agreed to go shoot a game of pool. I met him at a local sports bar. Albert was a handsome, thick brother that looked like he used to lift weights back in the day. He didn't look his age at all and his personality was cool. We hit it off right away. It was like he and I knew each other for a long time. Albert told me that he thought I was too good for Jesse and that he thought I should look elsewhere. He told me that Jesse told him all about me and the girls and that I deserved better. The first thing that came to my mind was that Albert was trying to make Jesse look bad because Albert took a liking to me. So straight off the back, I told him how I felt about Jesse and that I wasn't interested in looking elsewhere. Albert didn't look too happy about that. It was like it was all personal for him. He was actually trying to discourage me from Jesse. After being out for a few hours with Albert, we parted and went back to our homes. When I got in, the girls said that Jesse hadn't called or came by. I then called Rolonda and told her what my evening was like and she said to listen to Albert. She continually repeated herself about something not being right with Jesse. I started to see exactly what she was talking about.

Sunday rolled around and Jesse decided to show up. I asked him where he was all weekend and he told me that he went to a football game in Alabama and had his cell phone turned off. He said that he had it planned with a few friends from work and forgot to tell me about it. He continued to apologize, but that wasn't enough for me. I expressed to him how ignorant and inconsiderate he was and that I didn't think it would be a good idea for him to remain in my presence any longer. I packed Jesse's belongings and asked him to leave. He said that he would have to call Albert to pick him up. Instead, I drove him back to their house myself. The whole trip, Jesse sat in total silence. I told him that I thought it would be a good idea if he and I took a time out. He just looked straight ahead and shook his head in a nodding motion without words.

At that moment, I began to look at his age playing a big part in his actions. I wasn't use to that at all and wasn't about to deal with it. After I dropped him off, I went back home and explained to the girls that they wouldn't see Jesse for awhile. They were upset of course because they adored him, but my girls have such a mature attitude that they expressed to me that they were a little upset with Jesse as well for not showing up over the weekend. Seconds later, Albert called me. He was on the road to make a trip to Florida. He asked me if I heard from Jesse. I told him what went down and he said that I made the right choice. Albert stated that he didn't want to interfere, but it was just that he felt I was too good for Jesse. I told him about Rolonda and how the two of them shared the same advice. Albert asked me a few questions about Rolonda, showing an interest. I told him that they were the same age and that when he got back from Florida, I would show him a picture of her. He was all for that. In the mean time, Jesse honored my wishes and stayed away completely. I didn't hear a peep out of him or even an e-mail. Even though I told him that we needed a break, I still desired to hear from him.

CHAPTER *12*

Genesis 45:7 - But God sent me ahead of you to preserve for you a remnant on earth and to save your lives by a great deliverance.

It didn't take too long for the girls and I to get back into our routine of school and work. However, after being let go of from a job because of bankruptcy, I began working for another company. This time it was a "mom and pop" environment that I was using as a stepping stone until I got my company on its feet. I had been with the company for several months until they started losing clients, which meant they had to let go of some of their independent contractors. You know how it goes…last hired, first fired. This wasn't good at all. Robert wasn't paying any child support and I had no other means for income. My car payment was due again along with rent and everything else. My check only covered so much of my utilities. I made an attempt to call Robert and explained to him my situation. He stated that he didn't have any money and that he was advised by his lawyer not to pay me anything by ways of child support until he was made to do so. I was getting nowhere fast with him. He just didn't care.

While trying to find another job, the days were going by fast it seemed like. It didn't take long for the apartment office complex to tack a late notice on my door. I called and spoke with the office manager and explained to her my situation, of which she was understanding and gave me time to move out before she filed a dispossessory on me. I didn't know who to call. Here we were, being evicted with no place to go. We were homeless. I knew that I couldn't get another apartment in my name and lucked out with this apartment only because the leasing agent was a man that understood my situation and showed me mercy by not checking my credit. I began searching for apartments on the Internet. After making so many calls to complexes and being turned down, I saw no light at the end of my tunnel. Then I made an attempt at one more phone call to a complex that would only accept my application if I was making payments on an apartment that I was in the credit bureau for back in 1997 in Virginia Beach. So, I called the complex that put me in the credit bureau and asked them if they could give me a letter from their letterhead that stated that I would make payment arrangements. The office manager of the complex in Virginia Beach was so snotty and rude that she refused and advised me that the only way she would do something like that was if I made payment in full. I was getting nowhere fast with her as well, so I ended the phone call abruptly by hanging up on her.

I knew that I had to find some place for my girls and refused to lie down and cry about it. This complex was the only one that was going to give me a chance and all I needed was a letter stating that I was making payments to the old complex. I knew that there had to be some kind of way to make this happen, so I thought and I thought and came up with an idea of making up the letter myself. I went onto my computer and made up a letterhead with the apartment complex name in Virginia Beach and typed up my letter. I fixed my fax machine to the complexes fax machine in Virginia Beach so that when I faxed this information to the complex that I was trying to get into, they would see the Virginia Beach's letterhead and fax number come up. I knew it was a crooked thing to do, but I had to do something for the sake of my children. Nothing else mattered. With a lot of prayer and asking the Lord for forgiveness, it worked. All I had to do was get out there and fill out an application. I didn't tell them that I had just lost my job, so what I did was tell them my business company name and that I was self-employed. All I had to show was my last year's returns and we were in there. Now the hard part was who was I going to get to move us? The money I had from my paycheck was only enough to pay the first months' rent on our new apartment and the security deposit.

I called Albert to see if he would help me move to my new apartment and he stated that it wouldn't be a problem. I then called Rolonda and explained to her my situation and she said that she was glad that Albert would get me help, but to be careful with him too because he was still roommates with Jesse. I didn't want Jesse to know where I was moving to, so I asked Albert not to say anything about it. He agreed and promised to keep everything hush, hush for me.

As time went by, the girls and I were all settled in our new gated access apartment. It was a 3 bedroom, 2 bath, and very spacious place that only cost $675 per month. It was a great deal in a nice part of town out by Six Flags Park in Douglasville, Georgia. I landed a good job making $500-750 bi-weekly. Robert and I continued to stay in touch with one another. After paying my lawyer a little more, he put the pressure on Robert's lawyer to have him begin child support payments of $700.00 per month. We were living pretty well.

Months went by and Albert and I continued to be friends. We would go shoot pool together and drink a few beers. Our friendship was simply that...a platonic relationship. He was so cool. I especially enjoyed his old wisdom, but there was something quite strange about his always talking about Jesse. He and Jesse were still roommates, but Albert talked about kicking him out. He would also ask me if I heard from Jesse every time we got together, which was once in a while. I told Rolonda about it and she said that there is something going on there between the two of them. She was concerned for my welfare and said that she was coming down to stay with me for two weeks to "watch over me." When Rolonda arrived, I introduced her to Albert. Albert couldn't stop staring at her. It was as if he was mesmerized or something. He started talking about taking care of her and that he would give her anything she wanted. I was really tripping because this was his first time meeting my sister. I know she is pretty, but damn. She told me that she wanted to get to know Albert a little bit more because there was more to him than meets the eye. She believed that he wasn't all that I saw him to be and she was right. Albert and Rolonda made plans to have dinner at his house.

When the hour rolled around for their dinner date, it didn't happen. She called Albert and asked what was going on and Albert was quite hesitant on answering, so she just came right out and asked him if he was gay. I thought I would die. How could she think something like that about Albert? When asked, Rolonda motioned for me to pick up the other phone and to listen quietly, so I did. What I heard on the other end was devastating enough for me. Albert said yes, he was and that he and Jesse were together. That's why their dinner date never happened, because Albert and Jesse got into an argument over it. I hung up the phone and thoughts started going through my mind about Jesse. That's why he never touched me. That's why he would act irritated whenever I would try to cuddle with him. I thought he was just being a gentleman or that I was moving too fast. Here it was that he was gay. It was hard to swallow, but it all made sense. Rolonda ended the call with Albert by calling him a few choice words and hanging up on him. She said she knew something wasn't right about the two of them and that's why Albert was always talking about Jesse and asking me if I heard from him. She said they were involving me in a triangle. I was so thankful that she was there for me. I never would have figured that out and if in some kind of way I had, I don't think I would have balls enough to come out and ask Albert if he was gay. Rolonda was one that never bit her tongue about anything. I was more than grateful to my sister for rescuing me. I treated her with a bottle of wine and a platter full of shrimp that night. We sat up all night eating, drinking, and laughing at Albert and Jesse.

Several months went by and to my surprise; I received an e- mail from Jesse. Just out of the clear blue. He was the last person I expected to hear from. He stated that he and Albert were no longer friends and that he didn't understand what happened between us and that he was sorry and would like to come see me and the girls.

Apparently, Albert had kicked Jesse out and he needed a place to live. I e-mailed him back and told him that I didn't think it would be a good idea to come see us and that I didn't want to hear from him again. The nerve of him trying to come back into my life after the way he treated me. He was a liar, a user, and entered our lives under false pretenses. If he had gay intentions, then why bother with me. What an ass. I was glad that he was out of my life. At that moment, I vowed celibacy and not to talk to any guys under the age of 30. Jesse was a close call. I was grateful that we never had any sexual relations.

In the meantime, I was still receiving calls from Robert. He began telling me sob stories of how unhappy he was. I informed him that he needed to get his own place. He stated that it was in the making, but that he had to be careful because Felecia was crazy. He gave me Felecia's full name, her date of birth, where she worked, and her home address in case anything ever happened to him. He was truly upset and afraid of this girl, but this was what he chose over his wife and kids. I couldn't help him, except to repeat my idea of his getting his own place. After he gave me Felecia's information, he hung up abruptly because he heard her key in the door.

The next day, I upped his life insurance policy. It was an everyday ongoing thing for Robert, calling me 5 or 6 times a day. He would call when he was at work, going to the store, and when he had a moment alone in the bathroom, and he would whisper when the girl was sound asleep. He would call at 2 or 3 o'clock in the morning. I had enough of it. I told him to please stop calling me about this girl that he left his family for. I asked him if he had any type of remorse for his actions and he stated that he regretted it every day of his life, but I didn't believe that because when things were fine between them I never heard from him. It was like Dr. Jekyll and Mr. Hyde. He had too many faces for me, but when they fell out, he would dial my number like it was second nature to him. I would answer and listen because it made me stronger and I got a personal pleasure out of knowing that he was miserable, but even that got old. I was just completely fed up. I told him not to call me anymore. That only lasted for about two weeks. Robert called again, but only to say that he had gotten his own place and he gave me his new phone number and address.

Even though I had no more feelings towards Robert as far as us getting back together, I was glad that he had gotten his own place. He even started going back to church every Sunday. Now when Robert was with Felecia, he began sending little or no child support. After they broke up, he continued to be late or not send anything and it really didn't matter what the lawyers said, Robert was going to do what Robert wanted to do. By him being ignorant in that manner, this made me late on my car payment. My job was a fluctuating pay scale and didn't cover all my bills without the support payments.

When I informed Robert that I needed extra money sent and to take it out of the next payment, he said that it was fine and not a problem for him to do that. Then when the time came for the payment to be in my hand, I received a letter from my lawyer that was a carbon copy sent from his lawyer stating that "I attempted to extort money from his client (Robert) because I couldn't get it from any of my many boyfriends." I was so upset that I didn't eat for a week straight. All I did was cry so much that I carried a headache for over two days and that was with taking aspirin. I just couldn't believe it. Why would Robert tell his lawyer such a thing about me? I called Robert at home and told him that I got the letter his lawyer sent to mine and what it had stated and he claimed that he didn't know his lawyer was going to word it the way he had. What a terrible lie. I told him that it was obvious that he didn't want to pay the support and that I didn't want him calling me anymore. I didn't know what to do. It was a few weeks away from Christmas and I needed a vehicle for the girls. Not knowing how to go about dealing with the risk of losing my vehicle to repossession, I called a car dealer and confided in him about my situation. He informed me to not call the finance company and to meet him at his car lot in the morning. He told me that he could help me by trading it in. I believed him and trusted him. The next morning I went to meet this car salesman. I told him that it didn't matter to me what type of vehicle I got just as long as I could get something. With me trying to get a new car it meant that I wouldn't have a car note until a month afterwards, and by then my finances would have been in better shape, but the finance company couldn't wait that long unfortunately.

After being in his office well over three hours, he began speaking about the Bible and how much of a Christian he was and that he was going to help me out. Then he asked if I could meet him for lunch so we could further discuss how he could help me. This didn't sound right to me at all. I told him that it was okay if he couldn't help me and left his office. For a week straight, he would call my home and ask me to meet him for lunch so he could get me into a new car.

CHAPTER *13*

Genesis 9:3 - Everything that lives and moves about will be food for you. Just as I gave you the green plants, I now give you everything.

At this point in my life, I was completely fed up with brothas and their nonsense lies and messed up games. I couldn't believe this man that looked as if he had kids my age was trying to hit on me. I was at my wits end. After ignoring his phone calls shortly afterwards, I received a knock on my door around midnight. Of course, I didn't answer and wondered who it could have been because I knew of no one that would come to my door at that time of night. That morning when the girls got up for school, something told me to ask them if our truck was still outside and they informed me that it wasn't. That takes care of the mystery person knocking on my door that late. It was Mr. Repo man, coming to take my only means of transportation away. The first person that came to my mind was the salesman. He was angry with me because I didn't respond to his passes. My blood was boiling. I called him at work and told him thank you for taking the car away from my children and he replied that he was sorry, but he could help me if I would just listen to him. I didn't want to hear anything he had to say. I just wanted to call him and let him know that I knew what he did. The conversation ended with me hanging up on him. Then I called information and got his home number along with his supervisor's name and left messages with his wife of how much of a rotten husband she had and told his supervisor what a dirty low-down salesman he had working for him. Of course this wasn't the right thing to do, but it sure felt good. I had to resort to walking to the grocery store that was 2.5 miles away and taking a cab back because I didn't have enough money to take a cab to and from the store or to rent-a-car with. I felt like a failure to my girls. I didn't know what to do except to keep working and keep bugging my lawyer about getting Robert's wages garnished and my divorced finalized. In order to do that, I had to pay my lawyer. However, if I had to use what I made from my job to try to keep a roof over our head and pay utilities, how could I pay my lawyer if Robert wasn't paying the support at all? Or, when he did pay, he made the payments late on purpose.

At the end of the month, I was blessed with having a few extra bucks to be able to rent a car and buy the girls' Christmas gifts. It hardly amounted up to what they were used to getting, but being as understanding as they were and knowing our circumstances, they were grateful. We enjoyed our Christmas together as we managed to enjoy all of our days spent without a husband and a father. Robert never called on Christmas. He didn't call until a week later to ask what the girls wanted for Christmas. It disgusted me to no end. This time, I allowed the girls to tell them how they felt.

As each one got on the phone in our apartment, I removed myself and went into the bathroom so the girls could speak the way they wished. I didn't want to influence them in any way or make them think that they had to say what I wanted to hear, so I gave them their privacy, but I listened at the closed door. He must have asked the girls what they wanted for Christmas and our oldest spoke first and responded with she didn't want anything from him, but thanked him anyway. Then our middle child and the youngest told him the same thing. I know that his feelings were hurt to hear the girls talk to him like that, but I'm sure it hurt them more to tell him. Then our oldest spoke up and said "Mommy isn't even in the room." So I figured he stated to them that I told them to say those things.

A few months had gone by and I hadn't heard from Robert by way of telephone or child support, so it had been a struggle for us financially. I hadn't had a chance to get my company's commercial shown on air to try and build clientele because of the lack of money. Whatever I made from my current job barely covered my rent and utilities. It was pretty hectic and damn rough.

At those moments in my life, I knew that I was experiencing the true meaning of single motherhood, the one thing that I feared most. I became it and I didn't like it one bit. How was it that Robert could live so comfortably and the girls had to suffer? I couldn't even afford to buy them the type of clothes they wanted or shoes and sneakers…let alone under clothes. Food was another story. There were days that we didn't have too much of anything to eat. We were down to a half a meal a day. The girls were fine when they were in school because they had free lunch. They ate breakfast and lunch at school, but when they came home, there wasn't much to give. I survived off of water while they were in school. I tried to keep my mind off of being hungry by working and when I finished working, I started exercising. I tried to get myself in a mindset of being on a diet kick. Some days it worked and most days it didn't. I needed more help than what I was getting. I needed money.

I even thought about working outside the home, but that would take even more money because I had no transportation. Then the humiliating thought came across my mind of welfare. I cried just thinking about it. How did it come to this? It seemed like every time I tried to make a step ahead, I was pushed five steps back, always at the hands of someone else. I searched the white pages to find a social service office close to me. I didn't even know what to say to them when they answered the phone. All that came out was that I needed information on getting assistance. The woman on the other end told me what I needed to do and offered to mail me an application since I told her that I had no transportation. After I hung up the phone, I sat on my bedroom floor and cried until my head ached with excruciating pain. I couldn't look myself in the mirror with such feelings of failure for letting my girls down. Usually, at a time such as this with me feeling the way that I did, I would normally be on the phone crying my heart out to Rolonda or Janet, but I was far too embarrassed and ashamed. I started feeling sorry for myself, drowning my soul with questions on how someone that owned and operated a business for three years with a staff of 12 and a clientele of 15 making up to $75,000 a year came down to having to resort to welfare. I was angry and confused. It was to the point where my evenings and weekends boiled down to me getting the girls settled and making sure they were comfortable so I could go in my bedroom and cry. I felt peace by doing that. It was like I had a date with pain. I couldn't wait to go into my room, shut my door, and just let it all out with my Bible in my hand and me on my knees. There wasn't a day that went by that I didn't get on my knees and pour my heart out to the Lord.

Even though we were going through the most difficult time in our lives, I still felt a peace deep in my soul. When I tried to focus on where it was coming from, my spirit felt overwhelmed with a rush of air through my lungs that dried my tears. I didn't understand, but tried to interpret it as being strength from within my soul. I began to think that there was a light at the end of this tunnel. A strong bright light that was too distant at this moment to see clearly. To express what my heart was enduring, I began to write poetry on a daily basis. It got to the point that it seemed like the hard times would occur so often that I used up three legal pads writing about everything from the beginning of my life to the present. Writing became my comfort. It was my escape and I did it with such a passion that I would sleep with a pen and pad beside my bed in case I got an inspiring thought. I would take it with me everywhere I went, even to the grocery store.

A few days passed and I received the social service application in the mail. It looked like a small book that asked all kinds of questions about your personal business. Not having a choice, I filled out every question that applied to me. When it got to the part that asked are you receiving child support, I put no because I didn't want that to hurt my chances of receiving food stamps and Medicaid, for which I had applied. I didn't ask for any cash assistance because I knew that if they found out about my getting child support, whenever Robert sent it, they would either cut me in half or cut me off. I had Medicaid assistance before for our oldest daughter to cover the price of her medications, so I knew a little about how they worked.

48

After filling out the application, I noticed how close they were from where I lived, so I walked to the office the next day to return the application. They were about a half a mile closer to me than the grocery store was, so it wasn't a big deal for me to walk. After I got there, I took my application to the receptionist and had a seat. It only took about 15 minutes for someone to call me to the back for an interview.

When I actually got back there and sat down and took in my surroundings, I was trying hard to fight back the tears, but it was too late. I had hoped the woman interviewing me wouldn't notice, but I think she did. She never said anything about it. She just spoke softly and calmly to me as if she knew what my tears were for. I felt so humiliated and like a failure. At that moment, I hated Robert with a passion. I wanted to die. The interviewing process took about 30 minutes to an hour. It wasn't too bad, but that didn't help my heart from feeling low. They informed me that I would be receiving a letter in the mail letting me know if I was eligible and if so, how much I would be receiving in food stamps and when the Medicaid would go into effect.

When I left the office, I felt like, one down and many more to go. It was a relief being out of that office, but even more of a relief knowing that I'd taken care of what needed to be done. After I got home, I called Robert at work and asked him when he was going to send the support payment and he stated that he didn't have any money at this moment because he had to pay his rent and utilities. He also stated that he may be moving from his apartment because he just couldn't afford it. He was paying $400 a month, he had no car payment but had a car, and with him being a Field Engineer in Computer Repairs, he was hardly home to use any of his utilities. I didn't understand how he had no money when I was paying $675 per month, plus an additional $350 for my utilities and he was making $32,000 per year, way more than I was making. It was a struggle for me to do that, but with the help of the Lord and His blessing of having my mother and grandmother be able to help me out when they could, we were barely making it. Robert later said that he actually gave up his apartment to move in with another woman and her two kids. What a poor excuse for a man, a father, and a human being. He even stopped going to church. He acted as if he couldn't bear to be alone. He just had to have someone. I couldn't believe what my ears were hearing. I asked him when should I expect payment since he was supposed to send $350 on the 1st and $350 on the 15th of each month and it was already close to the 15th and I hadn't received anything for the 1st yet. He said to bear with him and that he would send it as soon as he could. Something told me not to count on anything for that month or even look forward to any of the other months. I told Robert I had to go because my blood was boiling so much; I knew that I would say something out of my character to him and end up regretting it later by means of his lawyer. He always managed to turn around anything I said to him and feed it to his lawyer and his lawyer would put it into a negative letter and send it to my lawyer. He was dragging his feet tremendously because I couldn't afford to pay him what I owed in order for him to take care of the wage garnishment first and the divorce second. It didn't matter how much I complained about Robert. The true fact was that money talked and I didn't have a pot to piss in.

Shortly after hanging up with Robert, I received a phone call from my oldest daughters' school principal stating that she was having a hard time staying awake in class. I assured him that all my girls go to bed on school nights at 8:30 P.M. Then it hit me, back in Virginia, she had to have home schooling because of her petit mal seizures that caused her to faze in and out while looking straight ahead and then put her to sleep. I asked him if she looked a certain way that either he or her teachers had noticed and he stated to me that they had noticed her looking that way. I told him of the situation in Virginia with the home schooling and how the State provided a teacher to come into our home to give her studies. He was so apologetic and offered to take care of the arrangements for her to be in home schooling, but they did not provide any teachers to come into the home. I had to do it myself. I figured that since I was already working at home, it would be convenient to do so.

49

After school, she came home with the necessary paperwork and a curriculum that had helpful centers of where you could order the home schoolbooks. I ordered from the A-Beka Curriculum. To me, they were the best and they taught not only middle school courses, but they also had religion mixed in with it. They were a costly bunch of books, but well worth it. Since she was in the 7th grade and only had three months left of school, I decided to teach her on the 8th grade level so she would be ready for the following year. I had to rearrange my schedule to working nights from 11P.M. to 7 A.M. and get up with her to start home school at 9 A.M. until the other two came home from school, which was around 3P.M. Then we would eat dinner and I would try and get in a few catnaps until it was time for me to get back to work again. It was pretty hectic and began to take its toll on me physically, but I had to do it. In between catching naps, I would find myself praying for strength and falling asleep talking to God. It was definitely an experience. I needed a break…a chance to exhale, even if it was just for a moment. Then my moment came when I got a telephone call from Janet. She said that she was going to drive down from Virginia to visit us. I couldn't wait to see her. I told the girls and they were just as excited as I was. I had so much to tell her, so much to share. She was my release, my confidant. Ever since I had gotten the call from Janet, we were counting down the days till her arrival. It boiled down to the day she was to come into town. I had taken a cab to the grocery store and bought us two bottles of wine and a platter full of 100 shrimp. Janet called on her cell phone and asked for the directions to our apartment. She made it.

The girls and I went outside to greet her when she pulled up. It was so refreshing to see her again. When Janet got out of the car, we all just embraced her at the same time. We went into our apartment and put her suitcase up in the closet and showed her around our home. She complimented me on how nice she thought our place looked. Our evening consisted of staying up all night talking, Janet, the girls, and myself. It was getting late and before we knew it, it was midnight and the girls decided to turn in. Just when they went to bed, I broke out the wine and the shrimp. The drunker we got, the more laughing we did. We talked about everything from John Pierce to Jesse, Robert, and the present. We really enjoyed ourselves. The next day, we were so worn out from the night before that we just lounged all that Sunday.

Chapter *14*

Psalm 68:3 - But may the righteous be glad and rejoice before God; may they be happy and joyful.

Being back on the grind with work and home school with my oldest child Monday morning, I was grateful to have Janet here with me. She was such a huge help. Janet gave me a break the whole week and taught the home school course for me while I took my time and concentrated on my work. I felt such a relief. My work week was very light within my household thanks to Janet. As the time grew near for Janet to go back to Virginia, she wanted for her and I to go out for the evening. We filled Friday and Saturday evening with things to do. Earlier that week, we took a breather and went to a poetry reading at a laid back type of atmosphere called Club Kaya on Peachtree Street in downtown Atlanta. Janet asked me to read one of my poems on stage. Being that neither her nor myself have ever been to one, I thought, what the hell. The worst they can do is boo me.

We got dressed and found our way to Club Kaya. When we got there, I had to put my name on the list to do a reading. I was so nervous. I never did anything like this before, but at the same time, I couldn't wait to get on stage and release my smooth flow of expression. After listening to a few brothas and sistas express themselves with their choice of words in poetry, my time to be on stage was getting closer and closer. Janet and I drank a few Grand Marnier's with orange juice. I needed to calm my nerves. Then before I knew it, the host announced that there was a virgin coming to the mic, so show her some love and welcome Precious Love to the stage. I was next to the last person to get up there. My heart was pumping and I was shaking. As I got to the microphone on stage, I saw nothing but bright lights in my face. They were so bright that I couldn't see the audience. There was a live band and they played soft jazz while I recited my poem that I had worked so hard and long to memorize. The atmosphere and mood was nice and laid-back. With quivering in my voice, I began to recite. I guess the audience could tell that I was nervous because I heard a voice say, "It's all right, take your time." For some reason, I felt better. It was like they were really in tune and interested in what I had to say. Getting close to the middle of my poem without the quivering voice, I began to flow as if I was up there on stage reciting every night. The audience was feeling me because in between words, I heard, "That's right" and "Go ahead." It was a wonderful feeling. When I finished, all I heard was whistles from way in the back of the room and applause that drowned out the band on stage. That was a night I never forgot. As I stepped down, all I could think about was coming back to read again and again. I loved that response and I had to get more of it. That was me. I felt so at home and stress free.

As I got back to my seat, Janet gave me so many compliments. She was like "They were really feeling you." It was definitely an experience to remember. As the time got close for us to leave the club, we started on back home. I dreamed of my moment all night long. The next day, Janet was going to head back home to Virginia, but I convinced her to stay another night so we could catch a live show from Shang, the comedian at the Fox Theater in downtown Atlanta on Peachtree Street. I told her the way I found about Shang's show was that I went to www.bet.com to look up their online poetry contests and when I did, I saw a banner at the top that was Shang's. I clicked on it and it brought me to his web site. I remembered seeing his face, but never knew his name. I searched all through his web site and saw his itinerary and noticed that he was going to be in town. I searched a little more and read one of his poems and being that I was a poet myself, I e-mailed him and told him that I enjoyed his poem and asked if I could meet him. Two days later, I received a response and it was from Shang himself.

51

At first I didn't believe it. He said how much he appreciated my compliment. He then asked for my address so he can put me on his mailing list. I was hesitant because I wasn't sure if it was really him or not, so I declined. He then sent a response to my declination and stated that he wasn't a crazy person, but it was really him e- mailing me. I then gave my address and a week later, I received a postcard from his place of business in California. I then continued to write Shang and he responded to every e-mail I ever sent. He was such a real down-to-earth brotha. He was more of a philosopher to me then a comedian. He informed me that he had a CD out called, "Shangry." I immediately went out to buy that CD and told him that I would come to his show with it in my hand and walk up to him, so he would know who he was e-mailing.

The night came for us to go to the show. Janet was late as usual in getting herself ready. That girl would be late for her own funeral. When she was done, the girls complimented us on how pretty we looked. I was more than ready to go. I couldn't wait to get there and see him in person. After we finally got situated in parking and walked half a block to the show, we found a few seats open that were in the back, but not too far from the stage. Shang was the second performer to come on stage. When I saw him, my first thought was, "Damn he's fine"...he was more handsome in person than he was on his web page. Just like when he is on television, he knocked it out the box. He was so funny. After the show, I remembered he said that he would have a stand trying to promote his CD, so I got up to look for it and I saw him standing out in the hallway with fans surrounding him for his autograph. I waited until I could see that he had at least a second alone and walked up to him and held my CD out for him to sign. He looked at me, and then he looked at the CD, and then embraced me with the nicest hug. He said, "I know who you are." He proceeded to tell people, whom I thought were agents of his that we e-mail each other. He was so nice and not stuck up in anyway whatsoever. He signed my CD with "Wassup with your e-mailing ass." He then kissed me on the cheek and said to call him. I took that as stay in touch via e-mail, which we still do. I didn't know which night was my favorite, the night I read my poetry on stage or meeting Shang. I treasured them both.

CHAPTER *15*

Genesis 11:6 - The LORD said, "If as one people speaking the same language they have begun to do this, then nothing they plan to do will be impossible for them.

As morning came, Janet announced that she had to get going. The girls and I really enjoyed her company. I hated to see her go. I appreciated everything about her. I was grateful for our friendship and all the help she had given me ever since we met. She was a true friend indeed. After awhile, everything went back to our normal routine with home schooling and work. My stay in Georgia so far had been a pleasure, in spite of what the girls and I encountered during our first six months there. Those two exciting nights made up for it. As the months went by, Robert and I continued to correspond. He stated that he would like to come visit us. I told him that it would be fine with me, but that I had to check with the girls first to see how they felt about that. I went to talk to the girls and they said that they didn't mind, but they didn't want him to stay for too long. They also made sure to tell me to not allow him to sleep in my bed, but to sleep on the couch. I called Robert back and told him what the girls said and he informed me that he would catch a flight on our oldest daughter's birthday and stay for the weekend.

The girls and I rented a car and arrived at the airport, waiting for Robert's plane to land. I went inside and went to the service desk to ask if his plane had landed and before I could get an answer, Robert walked up to me. We hugged and kissed each other on the cheek. It was nice seeing him again. We walked outside the airport towards the car and the girls got out to hug him. Robert put his suitcase in the trunk of the car and the girls started telling him all about school and their friends. He seemed to be really excited about being in Georgia and seeing the girls again. As we pulled up into the parking lot of our apartment, Robert complimented us on how nice our complex was and when we actually got into our apartment, he commented on how beautifully I had it set up. The girls took them to each of their rooms and then we all ended up in mine. He started unpacking the gifts he brought for them and informed me that he was taking me out to buy my gifts. Before we could get out the door to go sightseeing, my phone rang and it was his new girlfriend Rachel. She wanted to speak to Robert and to see what he was doing. The girls and I left the room to give him his privacy and I heard Robert yelling at her. He came out and said that he would talk to me about it later. Afterwards, we all went to the Martin Luther King Memorial where we took Janet when she came to visit. He loved it and I just couldn't get enough of it.

Every time I went, it brought tears to my eyes. While walking up the sidewalk to visit Martin Luther King's home, our eldest daughter found $60 lying on the sidewalk. Robert stated that a tourist must have dropped it, but it didn't stop us from going out to eat with it. What was left of the money, he divided between the girls and myself. After lunch, we decided to go sightseeing. I can remember thinking that it was just like old times with having Robert with us again. It was as if he never left. We went shopping and Robert went all out and bought me all kinds of gifts. We were getting along so well. It felt quite comfortable and the smiles on our faces were no end. However, we were brought back to reality after we got back to the apartment when my phone was ringing off the hook with his girlfriend on the other end. I allowed myself to enjoy the moment of indulging in his kindness, but was relieved of how our situation was at hand. I enjoyed my freedom and was glad that he and I were not together anymore. I didn't mind Rachel calling because that only added to my strength. She showed me how insecure she was.

To most women in my situation, it wouldn't even have gotten this far, but I look at those things and brush them off. It's all drama to me and I don't allow that to penetrate into my life. I was much better than that and too damn cute to worry about it. Robert pretended that Rachel got on his nerves, but I knew that he cared for her because when I would be in another room, I could hear him talking sweetly to her. I was glad that he found someone. That way he could keep his mind off of trying to get back into my life. He mentioned getting back together on several occasions even before he came to visit. He asked if he could come to Georgia to live so we could be a family again, but I declined. I told him that I thought he should stay with Rachel. Of course, he was quite surprised about my statement, but it was all true. I was enjoying my freedom and didn't want to be tied down again, especially to him and all that he had inflicted upon me over the past years. Plus, our daughters weren't too keen on the idea of having him back in our lives in that way again. They would bother me with questions of when I was going to get married again and they used to tell their friends that they didn't have a dad. My poor babies. They were hurting and reaching, but I had no one decent in my life after our separation to fill that void for them or myself, but I knew that someone was out there for me. I was just tired of looking because when I did, I came up with momma's boys and liars like Karl and Jesse. It was too much for me, so I vowed celibacy and decided that if the Lord had someone for me, then he would be placed before me when the time was right.

Monday came and it was time for Robert to catch his flight back to Virginia. The girls said their goodbyes that morning before they went off to school. I then took him to the airport where we said our goodbyes with embracing and kisses on the cheek. Our visit was very enjoyable. I loved Robert, but he could never be my husband again. Months went by and he continued to call and speak sensibly. With his hopes of us getting back together, it seemed like anything that I needed financially, he would give without hesitation along with the child support. I appreciated it and felt that the extra was owed to the girls anyway and that's exactly what I did with the extra money. I spent it on my babies for their school clothes and supplies. I took whatever extra he wanted to give, even when I didn't really need it. Family members thought that I was crazy to continue communication with Robert, but they just didn't understand that I needed to do this so I would be able to get the girls the things they needed until our divorce was final along with his wage garnishment.

So far, so good - life in Georgia was great living. The girls were happy, which made me overwhelmed that they were all aglow. Everything was going great and I even landed a great new job in my field, this time with a large hospital in Fayetteville, Georgia. They offered more in wages and benefits and I was still working in the comfort of my own home. It was nice and I was satisfied. Nothing could be sweeter. I had plans on getting my business back on its feet with pricing air time rates to have my company commercial shown throughout Metro Atlanta. The girls remained honor roll and my life was drama free. Then finally, I had some peace of mind. Blessed is how I was living.

However, you know that you must be doing something right because the devil then finds some way to interfere. I received a call from one of my sisters named Rose from up home in Pennsylvania. She informed me that mother wasn't doing too well. Back in 1991, mother was diagnosed with Paget's disease, a deterioration of the bones that began in her head. It was beginning to take its toll on her by striking in her knees, causing osteoarthritis because she had no tissue in between her knees joints. Her bones were rubbing against each other, which caused a limp, and then it began in the other leg as well and started radiating up to her thigh.

Mother was a strong but stubborn woman that continued to work. She complained that she couldn't go out on disability because they wouldn't pay her as much if she was to continue working and SSI was difficult because just like disability, she would have to stop working completely. Then there were the physicians that stressed to mother that she needed to have a knee replacement, but with her being diabetic, she feared that she wouldn't heal properly, which was true.

However, she really didn't have much choice because if she didn't get the operation, then there was the chance of gangrene and then being wheelchair bound. Either way, it didn't look like a great outcome. It just looked to me that she was damned if she did and damned if she didn't. Of course, she refused the operation and continued to work. I then made the decision after discussing it with the girls about moving back up home temporarily for a year, along with the assurance that we were definitely coming back to Georgia to live. They seemed to like that idea because they loved living in Georgia just as much as I did. So it was a done deal. I informed my job what was going on with my mother and they told me that when I got back to Georgia, to give them a call because they had no problem with me working for them again. That was good to know. I now had a job when I got back to Georgia without the hassle of having to go through any changes in pounding the pavement and trying to find a job.

Shortly afterwards, I got in touch with a cousin of mine and a few friends to move our furniture into storage in Georgia. I then called to the schools up home that were close to where my mother was living so I could have the girls' schools in Georgia transfer their records. I went out and purchased airline tickets for us all to catch a flight to Pennsylvania. Lastly, I informed Robert of what was going on and he seemed to be sympathetic. I felt that I had to let him know where the girls' were going to be since he was still their father. I called Rosa and told her of the changes I made and that I was coming to help out with mother. I figured that I could take up some of the slack of mother having to work and be on her feet by being there and running errands for her, cooking, and cleaning. Plus, I had already set up a job doing the same thing in home with a little mom and pop shop to help financially. Robert was still paying the child support so that helped a lot as far as still being able to take care of the girls. Working 3rd shift was cool for me because I had to keep my mornings open in case someone needed me besides mother like my grandparents, who only lived over the hill, or the girls while in school.

It was time for us to leave and my cousin Gino and his wife Alicia took us to the airport. We had so much luggage that they had to bring both of their vehicles to transport us along with our suitcases. When we got to the airport Gino and Alicia saw us off to the plane. It was the girls first time flying and I was anxious to see their reaction when the plane took off. Fortunately, they got the chance to sit together with me across the aisle from them.

They just couldn't stop looking out the window at the clouds. I tried not to laugh too hard at them, but it was great to see their little faces all lit up and excited about an airplane ride. We had a four hour long flight to Pennsylvania. When we arrived, there was mother and Aunt Ellen waiting for us. It was so nice to see them since I hadn't seen mother since she moved back up home from Virginia. We only talked over the phone. When I laid eyes on her, it saddened my heart. She didn't look in the best of health and her limp was awful to witness. I knew then that I made the right decision to come back and try this all over again with taking care of her since it didn't work out too well in Virginia with Robert.

After we left the airport, we went to Mother's home and got settled in. My grandparents came over to visit and brung some goodies as usual. The girls loved it. Mother only had a one bedroom apartment so I slept on the couch and my middle one and eldest slept on an air mattress while my youngest slept on a cot in mother's room beside her bed. She talked about getting a 3 bedroom apartment, but I informed her that we would only be staying until the girls got out of school, which was for approximately 10 months. I offered for her to come back to Georgia with us to live so we could get a house for us all and live comfortably. That way, she could go on disability, get her operation, and finally be able to enjoy the rest of her years in peace. She said that she would give it some thought.

After spending several weeks there, living up home wouldn't be as bad as I had thought it would be. It didn't take me long to get my wheels turning as far as my company went so I called the local television stations to get air time rates to have my commercial shown. My goal was to open up my business again in Pennsylvania, then get it established by having my sister Rosa work for me as an independent contractor, as she was taking courses in my field. Then as things progressed more, I would hire more independent contractors and leave this for Rosa to take care of while I would be back in Georgia setting up shop there as well. I had so much time on my hands in the mornings that I could do nothing but plan ahead for our future.

CHAPTER *16*

Proverbs 25:15 - Through patience a ruler can be persuaded, and a gentle tongue can break a bone.

As time went by I began thinking about Thomas Howard again. I decided to get in touch with him since I was going to be in Pennsylvania for a while. I called information to try and get his number and they told me that two numbers with that name were non-published and they proceeded to give both numbers with that name that were published and I decided to dial the first one given. A man answered and right then I knew it was Thomas, but I asked if it was Thomas Howard anyway and he said yes. I told him who I was and with excitement in his voice, he said, "Wassup cutie, where you at?" I was surprised, as I didn't know how he would take me, but he seemed just as excited to hear from me as I was to speak with him. He asked if I was still in Virginia and I informed him that I was in town and the first thing he said was that he was coming to get me. Just hearing his voice took me back to when we were together. Thomas was always a special man to me. He never put his hands on me. He was sensitive, sweet, understanding, and caring. I always loved Thomas and regretted our break up for many years.

Thomas was four years older than I was. We were together for 2.5 years, and then I met Robert. However, that wasn't the cause of our break up. Thomas cheated on me and told me about it, but we still didn't last. Here I was for 15 years enduring nonsense from Robert, but I stayed for my children's sake. Thomas, he at least was man enough to tell me what he did and I let him go anyway. I was so young and dumb. I was not quite a teenager when Thomas and I first met. After talking for a few hours, Thomas informed me that he had just gotten out of a 7 year relationship that ended with his mate walking out on him to be with another man. Our situations were similar in some ways, except Thomas was never married and he didn't have any children. He asked me if I could have more babies and I told him of my desire to want a son, but that I would have to find my next husband in order for that to take place. I told him that I was celibate and did not wish to make love to another man unless it was someone that I was sure that I was going to spend the rest of my life with. He said that he wanted a boy and a girl. He seemed to overlook what I said and proceeded to ask where was I exactly because he wanted to see me. I gave him the address and directions as Thomas was approximately 90 miles away from me, him being in Allentown and I in Harrisburg. I couldn't wait to see him again. We e-mailed each other a few pictures of ourselves to let one another know how we looked in our present lives. He said that he gained a few pounds and he may not look the same to me. I informed him that I had gained a few pounds myself after having three children. When I got his pictures from my e-mail, he asked if I was still down with our afternoon meeting, I told him that he was just as handsome as I remembered. After viewing my picture, he stated that he really had to see me now.

Thomas called off work where he is a Locomotive Engineer to spend the rest of the day and evening with me. I spent the last few hours primping and awaiting Thomas's arrival. When he arrived I ran up to him with open arms and he was all smiles, greeting me with a kiss on the cheek and saying "Hey pretty face." He always called me that. We held each other so tightly. I couldn't believe he was right in front of my face. He really was just as handsome as ever. I brought him inside to re-introduce him to mother, as they remembered each other from our past, and I then introduced him to my girls as I had told them about Thomas when we were in Georgia. I informed everyone that Thomas and I was going to be out for a while and that I would be back late. As we were walking out, he handed me his car keys, insisting that I drive. We were heading out on the highway back to his place and Thomas couldn't keep his eyes off me. We stated how nice it was to see each other after all these years. He kept kissing my hand continuously as I drove with the other. I felt so comfortable with him.

As we were approaching his home, he decided to take over the driving so he could show me around Allentown. Then finally, we pulled up in the driveway of his apartment. Thomas had a nice little pad, neat and clean, just as I had expected. He walked me through his apartment and then we sat on the couch to get more comfortable. We talked about our pasts to each other. Thomas asked if I was divorced as of yet and I informed him that I was not, but that I had to make a trip back to Virginia to get that taken care of the first week of the following month along with wage garnishment.

I told him about the abuse I endured, both physical and mental, and he proceeded to tell me about his ex-girlfriend - they were only broken up for 5 months at this point in time. He said that it still bothered him, which I truly understood. I could see that Thomas was still feeling the pain, but that didn't stop him from expressing himself to me. He said that there was always a place in his heart for me. He stated that he was trying to get in touch with me when I was in Virginia through my e-mail address, but by that time it had changed. I always loved him. He was my first love. Here I was in his presence, in his apartment, back into his arms again. As time got later and later with our long conversations, he asked me to stay the night. At first, I was hesitant because we hadn't seen each other in over 16 years and with our situations being what they were, I wanted to be careful in regards to us being on the rebound and destroying what we were developing. We expressed wanting to be together again and that my having children didn't matter to him. He just asked that I be patient with him in removing what was inflicted from his past. I told him that I would because I thought he was well worth the wait. He told me how great I made him feel as far as being wanted and desired. It was as if he was reading my mind. He made me feel beautiful and like a woman again. I wanted nothing more than to make love to Thomas. I reminded him of my celibacy for close to two years and that I hadn't been touched by a man in that way since then. He assured me of his gentleness, we made our way back to his bedroom, and with such passion, we indulged in each other's essence and I exploded from the inside out. We slept till dawn.

The next morning after, we took our showers, we went out for a bite to eat, and Thomas couldn't seem to keep anything in his hands. He was fumbling everything he touched. He seemed to get irritated by his clumsiness. I asked him if everything was all right and he replied with, "I forgot to take my happy pill today." I was silent for a moment and asked him what he was talking about and he said he takes anti-depressants because he couldn't handle things too well and he "gets angry quick." Right then, a red flag went up with me in this regard. I started to see another side to Thomas, but commenced to telling him that he didn't need any anti-depressants and that he just needed someone to talk to, but he stared into space, gave no response for at least 10 minutes, and came back with that he was "a screw up and his priorities were not in order." All of a sudden, he wasn't Thomas anymore. Everything that I heard and saw the night before was a totally different personality then what was in my presence at that moment. I tried telling him positive things and offered my help as far as anything that he may have needed, but he refused me. The last 30 minutes of our ride back to my mother's home was spent with no words exchanged. We just listened to the music play. When we arrived, he said that he would call me later that evening, but for some reason, I didn't think that he would. I just thought that I would chalk it up without regret. The later it got, the more I was about to chalk up that encounter and then the phone rang. It was Thomas. He was at work on the train. We talked about the night before and then about work. We must have talked for at least an hour and a half. Before ending our phone conversation, he asked if I was sure that I was going to be patient with him and I gave him my word that I would be. He then ended the call with "I love you Precious." My heart dropped. I was going to tell him that I loved him, but he said it first. That meant a lot to me. I told him that I loved him too.

For the next two weeks, Thomas would call two or three times a day and we would occasionally catch each other online with instant messages. We would talk in the wee hours of the night when he had to work on the train. It didn't matter to me how late or early it was, I was anxious to hear from him. He filled me up and made most of my time spent in Pennsylvania pleasant.

It felt so good to have someone in my life again. I would question myself with was he the one and thinking that all this time in dealing with those two mishaps in Georgia and looking for "the one," here he was right in my own backyard. I called Janet to tell her what was going on with me and she just giggled, stating that she knew a man had to be involved because she hadn't heard from me since I got back to Pennsylvania. She said that Thomas sounded like an honest man and that she thought it was wise for him to wait before we got completely involved with one another until he was clear of his past. She said that gives me enough time to get my divorce settled with Robert and get my business back together. Janet was right in every way. In the meantime, my time consisted of taking care of my babies, working harder, pulling double shifts, and making sure mother was making all of her doctor appointments.

Shortly afterwards, the phone calls from Thomas ceased. I was beginning to wonder if everything was all right. It seemed strange to me for him to just stop calling all of a sudden, so I decided to call him. I called and called, no answer. I even e-mailed him and I received no response. So I took it as he wasn't ready to commit to me and I accepted it and decided that I was going to leave him alone. I figured that if and when he was ready to be with me, that he knew how to get in touch with me.

CHAPTER *17*

Hosea 9:11 - Ephraim's glory will fly away like a bird— no birth, no pregnancy, no conception.

I was determined to stay focused on what I had to do in order to make a better life for my girls and myself. My main objectives were to go to Virginia to get my divorce finalized, get wage garnishment (with child support arrears included) from Robert, then file bankruptcy to get my credit straight since our credit was combined. Nothing was going to get in my way. At least that's what I thought until a letter was sent home from school with my oldest daughter stating that they wanted me to pay $35.00 per day for my three children to go to school from September 21, 2001 to November 1, 2001. They didn't consider us living with my mother as a permanent address because our names weren't on her lease. Our plan was to stay with my mother until June when the girls got out of school because we were going to move back to Georgia and have mother come with us. That way I could take better care of her in regards to her health, but in the meantime, we were planning on moving into a 3 bedroom, 2 bath apartment on November 1, 2001. Then our names would have been on a lease, but they couldn't wait until then. They wanted me to pay a total sum of a little over $2000 in tuition costs for my girls to attend their public school ASAP.

Being that the neighborhood where my mother lived was predominantly white, there were some prejudiced individuals and we were no exception to their ignorance. It didn't matter to them that my girls were honor roll students with perfect attendance. They stated that they were going to withdraw them unless I agreed to pay and I was not about to pay them anything when my girls were attending a public school. To bypass their ignorance, we decided to move to my grandparent's home 10 minutes from my mother's apartment, but they were in a different school district. Grandmother and I went to the schools in her area and presented to them a notarized letter from her stating that the girls lived with her. These people gave us no problem, we enrolled the girls, and everything went well. The girls were more comfortable at the new school and I had peace of mind. It seemed that everything was getting back on track just fine until I realized that I had a whole month of not having my period. I thought that maybe I just had an irregular month for some reason, but days went by and nothing came about, except for some extremely tender nipples.

After not hearing from Thomas for a while, I wasn't too sure of his reaction to my news, so I decided to e-mail him what I had learned. Within 15 minutes, I got a phone call from him asking if I had a minute to speak with him. With much needed privacy, I took the phone call outside on the cordless. He asked me if I was for sure that I was pregnant and I assured him that I was. He asked if I had gotten a pregnancy test and I informed him that I had not, but that I would take one to be positive. However, I knew that I definitely was. My breast nipples were never tender and sore before I got my period and I was never irregular in my months, but I told him that I would call him in a couple of days to let him know. I also told Thomas that I was thinking about having an abortion if I was pregnant, but he didn't want to hear that. He stated to me how badly he wanted to have children and that he didn't agree to me aborting what he pertained to be "his baby." Then he confessed to me that the reason why he hadn't called in a while was because he didn't know if he wanted to be with me or not and that he was confused. He assured me that it had nothing to do with his ex-girlfriend because he didn't want anything to do with her anymore. He stated that I just "popped" back into his life after all these years and he felt pressured. I told him that I understood, but I wasn't so sure that I did. I just didn't want to fly off the handle and say something that I would have regretted later.

I tried to understand where he was coming from. I mean, I wasn't on welfare, I worked my ass off with pulling double shifts, I still had a business I was attempting to get back on its feet, I wasn't a club hopping hootchie or a gold digging ho, and I damn sure wasn't ugly.

I was an intelligent, strong black woman with a good head on her shoulders and a blessed, loving heart raising my daughters on my own and keeping focused on being a good mother. That's why I was upset by his statement. I then informed him that I was going to go back to Georgia sooner than planned. I told him that my girls and I would be leaving before Christmas, when the snowstorms came to Pennsylvania. I didn't have any intentions on telling my family members what was going on with me in that way. I was always a private person and I wanted to deal with this on my own. I wanted to get back to my peace of mind in Georgia. I told Thomas that I would call him in a few days to let him know if the test was positive or negative. I then used the excuse of the schools giving me such a hassle about the tuition still, even though the girls were out of that school district, that I didn't think it would be a good idea if we stayed. She said that with us leaving this soon, she wouldn't be able to go back to Georgia with us. I had hoped she wouldn't at this point because I didn't want to tell her that I was pregnant.

I decided to make a few phone calls to apartments and house rentals in Georgia to see what I could get as far as getting a roof over our heads. I also applied for another job there because you can never have enough money, especially if I decided to keep the baby, which I really wanted to. But I kept thinking about Thomas and how heavy he was into his antidepressants. I didn't want to chance some kind of birth defect.

I had my plans all laid out for me without losing focus on my main objective. I was going to drive to Virginia to get my divorce and wage garnishment finalized, file for bankruptcy, and move back to Georgia with or without a newborn baby. With Robert still hot on my trail as far as trying to get back together with me, I made up my mind to keep him in the dark about my situation with Thomas. My business was none of his business anymore. Besides, he was engaged to be married to Rachel. What a damn snake. I was so glad to finally be rid of him in just a few weeks. I informed the girls that we would be moving back to Georgia and they were just as excited as I was. I thought that I would spring the whole baby thing on them after we were settled because my youngest couldn't keep any secrets like the two oldest could.

Later on in the evening, I decided to e-mail Thomas and express myself in regards to his statement of him being confused on not knowing if he wanted to be with me or not. I just had to let him know that I didn't need him to be a stand in for anything as far as my children and myself were concerned. I was doing quite well in taking care of my babies and I certainly was not depending on him to take up the slack. With us both being AOL members, I could tell if he read the e-mail I sent him. It took a few days, but he read it. Of course, I didn't hear a response. I really didn't expect to. I just wanted him to know that I wasn't going to chase after him and I damn sure didn't want to appear like a needy single parent. I didn't need Thomas, but it sure would be nice if he decided to give himself to me completely. However, I was not about to beg. No man is worth that. I learned my lesson from Robert. I was strong enough in all aspects to take care of this new baby. I was excited, but on the other hand not too sure if I wanted to go through with it. I had mixed emotions. Then I allowed myself to indulge in the reality of actually having another baby. All I could think about was having my son. That sounded so good. My son. My baby boy. I couldn't imagine what he would look like. I just prayed as I did with my girls that he would be a healthy, happy, beautiful baby, just like my girls. God is good.

The weekend was here and Thomas was waiting on me to call him and let him know if the pregnancy test that I told him I was taking was positive or not. I decided not to call. I would much rather have him call me. After his little statement of feeling "pressured," it kind of made me look at him differently. I certainly wasn't going to call and look even more like I'm rushing him to make a decision. At this point in time, I really didn't care what he thought or how he felt. I didn't need him. All I needed was what was already in my life and that was God and my children. I was happy and content. Later on that evening, Janet returned my phone call after I left her a message telling her that it was very important that I spoke to her and to call me right away. When she called, after being so used to me having a "drama life" as she referred to it, the first thing she said to me was "What is going on now?" I asked her, "What does it mean when your nipples are tender?" and she replied with, "You have your period?" and I told her that, "I haven't seen mine in a month." She said, "No, you lying?" I told her that I was very serious and that Thomas was the father. She asked if I was ready for this and I told her that we were more than happy about it, but that I didn't know the status as far as he and I were concerned, but I really didn't care.

Something deep down inside was leading me to believe that this is the son that I desired to have and I'm not about to give up that opportunity. Thomas may be a confused brotha right now, but his genes along with his personality before the anti-depressants were top notch. He was a good guy. Everything I would want my son to be. To know how to treat a woman, to open the door for a lady. I felt blessed. My girls were already going to be just like their mother. Good heart and strong mind. My son would make my family complete. Janet stated to me that if anyone could handle a situation such as this, it would be me. She complimented me on my inner strength for being able to get through living with the type of pain I endured with Robert. I love Janet for that. She let me know that my heart really did shine through. I'm glad it was recognizable. That's how I knew that Thomas had a problem within himself. It had nothing to do with me.

It was obvious that he had been taking those antidepressants for quite a long time and he was right...he did need to get his priorities straight. I decided to call Thomas anyway. I told him that I was definitely pregnant and I heard his voice in a whisper say, "Yeah." I was just as happy as he was, but I played it off and asked what the problem was. He asked me if it was all right about me having the baby and I told him that if it was all right with him, then it was certainly all right with me. He assured me that it was and stated that we definitely needed to talk. He said that he would call me the next day. All night, I couldn't sleep a wink from thinking about what my future was going to be like. It was a lot to think about for sure.

I waited for Thomas to call me the next day, but I received no phone call. I decided to call him so we could discuss what was going to be done because I wasn't about to stay in Pennsylvania with a new baby. He answered, but the tone of his voice was different. Not pleasant at all. It was unlike anything I had ever heard from him before. It was as if he was out of character. He totally flipped the script on me. He started talking crazy like, "I could have been pregnant before I came to Pennsylvania" and that "he didn't think he could have any kids." It was almost like he had an audience, so he played the macho role. I tried so hard not to get upset at his terrible remarks and explained to him in a calm voice that I did not want to argue nor would I stoop to his level at making our conversation into a shouting match. He was silent. I guess he didn't expect my response to be so calm. I told him off in a nice sort of way and he just listened as I spoke. I proceeded with, "Don't flatter yourself into thinking that I would stoop as low as to getting pregnant on purpose to try and trap you." I reminded him of the fine brothas in Georgia with potential who were business owners, and even a few of my famous local buddies that I had the pleasure of spending time with in a platonic manner. I told him that if "I wanted to do anything like that, why would I choose you over them?" I certainly wouldn't come all the way from Georgia, pass over those type of brothas that I had no problem getting dates with, just to look him up from way back in his pissy little town to have his baby.

I also reminded him that I didn't come into town for him, that I was there because of my mother's health. Of course, this didn't set too well with Thomas. He cut me off with yelling about he didn't say that I was trying to do such a thing, it was just a thought he had, but I didn't buy that nonsense. I felt it never should have come out of his mouth, especially with him trying to belittle my character by showing his ass in front of whoever was at his apartment at the time. Later in the conversation Thomas let it slip that he was actually talking with another woman in regards to them having a relationship. I asked him why he neglected to tell me this in the beginning and he replied that, "he didn't have to tell me anything." Right at that moment, my heart dropped. I didn't feel anger, I just felt disappointed in his childish behavior. I had actually given him more credit than he deserved. I thought he was honest and true, but he turned out to be no different from the snakes that I had the misfortune of running into in the past. Hell, he was no better than Robert.

I didn't want to bite my tongue anymore and decided to release my actual thoughts and feelings and told him how wrong he was to lead me on with the "I love you's" and the talks about us being together that persisted in our late night phone calls. I told him that he made a change for the worse and I then apologized to him for the heartache that he endured from his past which turned him into the monster that he turned out to be. Of course, this didn't set too well with him either and he lashed out with harsh words about us not ever being together and that he would pay for the abortion, but he needed a couple of weeks to come up with the money. He said that he would call, but before he could finish his words, I just hung up on him.

For 15 straight minutes, I stood silent outside in the cold in total disbelief of what just took place. I didn't want to own that heartache, so I came to the conclusion to have ties cut completely with him and to go through with the abortion. I waited for a few weeks before I called Thomas back and told him that I was going to get the abortion, but I felt that because it took two of us to make this baby, that it was only fair that we split the cost. His voice seemed calmer and he was back to the man that I once knew, but I didn't allow that moment of civility to cloud reality. He was who he was…a completely different person with mental and emotional baggage and a bitter taste in his mouth. Thomas didn't speak much, except to say that when he came up with his half, he would call me in a couple of weeks.

Weeks and weeks went by and I was curious as to how far along I was because my jeans were getting tighter and tighter and I was feeling fatigued and nauseous. I finally called an abortion center that happened to be in Thomas's neck of the woods. It was the only place that performed abortions with a pill that caused you to have a miscarriage. Their prices were also reasonable so I made an appointment for the next day. I stayed up all night, replaying when I first called Thomas up all the way up to the present. It was still so unbelievable to me, the turn it took and how ridiculously out of hand it had gotten. I fell asleep dreaming of the whole incident, waking up with tears of disappointment. I suddenly began owning those feelings that I was trying to avoid. I certainly didn't need this type of heartache. I got up that morning with the same routine of seeing my babies to their bus stops and taking mother to work. I then continued on the highway to the abortion clinic, which took me approximately an hour and a half to get to. I filled out the paperwork and waited for them to call my name. While waiting, the waiting room began filling up with couples. Women with their significant others or husbands filling out paperwork for the same reason I was there. I was the only single person in the room. For a moment's time, I felt out of place and embarrassed. I had mixed emotions about the whole situation. I really wanted this baby and believed it to be my son, but every time I thought about Thomas, a part of me was glad to be at the clinic. I thought about the anti-depressants he was taking so heavily and I didn't want my son suffering from any birth defects because he didn't know how to get himself together.

My thoughts were interrupted with my name being called to the back for an ultrasound exam. Afterwards, I had to do the routine pee in the cup thing, and then they pricked my finger to get my blood type, and took my blood pressure. After all that, I had to go back out to the waiting room until my results were done. In the meantime, they called others to give them the same type of exam.

After everyone was done, they called me into the back again, but this time to deal with the financial part of the deal. The young lady informed me that I was too far gone (two months and four days) into my pregnancy. I asked how they figured that I was that far along. She stated that they calculate from the time I had my last period instead of the time of conception. I didn't qualify for the pill (non-surgical) form. I was so disappointed because I wanted to avoid the surgery to have the abortion, plus I was short $10.00. However, with a promise to pay, they allowed me to go for the surgery. The doctor who performed the surgeries wouldn't be on that side of town until late in the afternoon, and I didn't have time to wait, so I decided to go where he was to get it taken care of. The doctor just happened to be in New Jersey, which was approximately 20 minutes from my location. It was like the tail end of New Jersey. I couldn't get there fast enough. I had never been to New Jersey before, but I was on a mission and that removed the fear of driving there. At first, I thought about calling Thomas, but I didn't know how he was going to react and I didn't want any drama. I then drove to New Jersey and found the clinic in no time. I was scared about getting the surgery, but it had to be done. After waiting for 20 minutes, they called me to the back where I met the doctor. He was a gentle, soft spoken man that made me feel comfortable and talked his way through the surgery to make me even more comfortable and keeping my mind off of the pain. During the process, the pain wasn't too bad, but it was uncomfortable to the point where my eyes were beginning to swell with tears. It felt like a horrifying case of nonstop cramps with my legs wide open that I couldn't control and I tried to make it feel better by closing my legs and curling up in a fetal position with my moaning. It was a two minute procedure that felt like ten.

After it was over, I felt anger in regards to Thomas because of his awful attitude. I really wanted this baby. He was my son, but it just wasn't right. It was all wrong in terms of the timing, Thomas and I's status, and my reasons for being in Pennsylvania. I told myself that I would wait until I got married again to have another baby. I drove back to Harrisburg to pick my girls up from the bus stop and Mother from work. No one knew of what my day consisted of and I wasn't about to tell them. It was another ordinary routine day as far as they were concerned. I decided not to let Thomas know that I had already gotten the abortion because I didn't want him to think that he still didn't have to front for his half of the expense. However, I did call him a few weeks later and told him that I went to the clinic, but couldn't go through with the service because I didn't have enough money. He said for me to not worry about anything and that everything was going to be all right. He stated that he would call me in a couple more weeks because he didn't have any money for lack of work, but that he was starting back the following week. I thought to myself, "Now what if I was still pregnant?" Waiting on Thomas was only getting me farther along in the pregnancy. If I didn't know any better, I would believe that he wanted me to have the baby anyway. This only made me even gladder that I went through with the abortion. He was definitely mixed up and I didn't want any part of that with having a baby by him. His shoulders weren't strong enough for me. He had a weak mental status and I certainly didn't need that. As time continued to go by, Thomas kept putting me off with give him just two more weeks, but I would never hear from him unless I called within the two weeks' time whereas he would repeat himself. One part of me wanted to tell him that I had the abortion, but the other part of me didn't want to say anything because I wanted half my money back, which was only fair. I finally concluded that I was going to continue to try to get my money back and just leave him to believe that I was still pregnant. I planned that afterwards, if he finally came up with the other half of the money, I was going to tell him that I had a miscarriage. In the meantime, I worked on getting the baby weight that I gained shed off me with eating bran cereal for breakfast, lunch, and dinner. So far, I shed 5 pounds within Thomas's famous two weeks time slogan.

CHAPTER *18*

2 John 1:5 - And now, dear lady, I am not writing you a new command but one we have had from the beginning. I ask that we love one another.

As time passed by, Mother decided that she wanted to move to Georgia with the girls and me. She said that she was going to get her disability paperwork taken care of and as soon as that was done, she was free to go. I immediately got online and looked up 4 bedroom houses for rent and came up with an available home in Marietta, Georgia. After calling and speaking with the owner, he assured me that he was going to put an application in the mail. We planned on moving back after her doctor's appointments were taken care of, which was the second week in December. In the meantime, Robert had been calling continuously, stating that he wanted to know exactly when the girls and I were moving back to Georgia because he was going to leave Rachel to "get his family back" as he put it. He just didn't know that the girls no longer wanted a part in his life. His walking out on us and paying child support only when he desired really hurt their little hearts. They actually wanted me to have their last names changed to my maiden name. After giving that much thought, I decided to have their names hyphenated with my last name and Robert's. That way, they can go by either one of their choice instead of taking his name off completely. I don't know why I continued communication with Robert. I already knew what a snake he was and the many faces he had shown. I guess I felt sorry for him in a way, because he was lost mentally and spiritually. I think he actually believed the lies he told his family and our friends about me taking the girls and leaving him instead of the truth of him walking out on us for another woman and her children. He was a lost soul that refused to look in the mirror to see what really was. A coward trapped in his own ignorance. He actually believed that because I forgave him for walking out on us that it meant the girls felt the same way. I loved Robert. He was my husband for 15 years, but he could never be my husband again. I dealt with the cheating and the baby by Dana, which was bad enough, but for him to actually walk out with no remorse or sensitivity at all is unlike anything I had ever dealt with or heard of before. Robert kept saying that he would do anything to make my life a lot easier and take care of me better than he had, but he never mentioned anything about the girls. That's what bothered me so much. These were his own children. He was in the birthing room with me through all three pregnancies. He had the joy of watching his own children being born, but as soon as a piece of ass came along, he was on the first thing smoking. I don't blame the girls at all for not wanting anything to do with him. They often told me to stop talking to him. When we moved to Georgia, they didn't want him to have our address or phone number. My babies...I can learn a lot from them. They are strong-minded little ladies that make me proud. Robert would tell me that he loved me and stated that if he and I didn't get back together that he was never getting married again. What a bunch of nonsense. He had already told some mutual friends of ours that he was engaged to Rachel. I mentioned that to him and he said that she was in for a rude awakening, that her children, little bastards as he put it, were not his kids and he really didn't care for her. He was only there to get what he could get financially. He was such a sorry ass man. All I had to say to him was, "Come on home, Robert" and he would leave that girl just like that. He was no good and would never change. If things were going fine between the two of them and he actually got what he wanted from her, then he would refrain from speaking rude about her and I wouldn't hear from him.

Robert wasn't fooling me at all. I knew that he was really engaged to Rachel because his lawyer pushed for our divorce more than my lawyer did. He paid his lawyer faithfully and that's why we didn't receive child support payments most months.

It didn't bother me that he was going to marry Rachel because I knew what a demon seed he really was and she wasn't getting anything special. If he walked out on his own family of fifteen years for a piece of ass, then he was capable of anything, but she didn't know this. He lied to her just as he did to his family members, his lawyer, and our friends.

November 1, 2001 was our commissioned hearing date to have our divorce finalized and wage garnishment taken care of. Robert showed up, but I couldn't make it. The hearing was in Virginia and I had too much on my plate with the girls, Mother, and myself. I called my lawyer the day after and asked what the outcome was. He sent a message through his secretary that everything went along smoothly and our divorce decree would be granted within three weeks and the garnishment would start shortly after. I wasn't happy with that at all. Robert did it to me again. He got away with an uncontested divorce instead of grounds of abandonment and he wasn't forced to pay the arrears on the child support. My lawyer wasn't much of a help and it really didn't matter if I showed up to the hearing or not. I felt like I couldn't win no matter what. I decided to call Robert to see if he was still going to send the child support, but pretended that I didn't know anything about how the court case went and he talked to me like I was a guy because Rachel was in the car with him at the time. I told him that I just wanted him to say yes or no if he was still going to send the child support for this month and he ended the call with, "I'll talk to you later brotha" and hung up on me. I took it as he was in his glory and he wasn't thinking about paying the child support for the month until he was made to through the wage garnishment. My heart was hurting with tears in my eyes, and I was getting furious so I turned to my Bible as usual and just started reading until I fell asleep. The Bible and praying was always my escape from hurt and anger. I didn't want to own those feelings, so this was my way of releasing them.

In the Bible passage of Proverbs, Chapter 11:21, it reads, "You can be very sure that the evil man will not go unpunished forever. And you can also be very sure that God will rescue the children of the godly." Proverbs Chapter 26:15, "Be patient and you will finally win, for a soft tongue can break hard bones." After I woke up, I felt relief, as if a burden was lifted. I had peace of mind. I looked at those verses and pertained them towards Robert and myself and just put it all into God's hands. Even though it looked like Robert was getting away with everything, he really wasn't. He was actually digging more of a hole for himself, but couldn't see it. God was in total and complete control. Robert had his new family, was engaged to be married, living quite comfortably, and even went as far as being baptized a second time, once with the girls and I and then again with Rachel, but he wasn't fortunate at all. He felt like he was on top and winning, but I was really the blessed one. The girls would always tell me to find someone else to marry. I let them know that it wasn't that easy to just find a husband and live happily ever after. Dating was a job within itself and I really had too much on my plate to invite someone into my space at this moment. I had the responsibility of taking care of them, as well as tending to mother in regards to her health. Then I still had to take care of me and I had plans of rebuilding clientele for my business. There was no end to my responsibilities.

Since I knew that mother made up her mind to live with us in Georgia, I began sending our resumes to open positions via e-mail. Even though mother finally received her disability, she still wanted to work at least part-time in Georgia. She was ready to leave when I was ready to go, and I planned on being in Georgia for Christmas. In the meantime, with all the planning, we still were awaiting an answer of approval from the house in Marietta. We sent the application back to the owner a week before. I began thinking that since the time was coming close to us being Georgia bound; I decided to continue calling Thomas for his half of the abortion money. I decided to leave Thomas an angry e-mail, as well as an angry message on his voicemail stating that he was going either to front the other half for the cost or pay a lot more later for 18 years in child support. If I knew that I had to be a bitch to get his attention, I would have talked to him like that from the beginning. He called within an hour of my voicemail message.

Thomas said that he still didn't have the money. He even had the audacity to suggest that I pay for the abortion now and allow him to repay me later by mailing it to me in Georgia. He must have taken more doses than prescribed in order for him to let some nonsense like that come out his mouth. All I could do was chuckle, which he didn't find too amusing.

I calmly let him know that the next time he promises to get in touch with me in 2 weeks time and doesn't, that he would be sorry. I couldn't believe the attitude I received from him, what an asshole. If that is the way I have to talk to men to get them to act civilized, then I don't need them. That is a sign of weakness to me and the more I think about Thomas, the better I feel about having had the abortion. I would much rather wait for my next husband to add another addition to my family.

A few days later, I received a call from the owner of the house in Marietta. He said that we were approved to move in. With much thought, I decided to call a special friend of mine back in Georgia named Lawrence Haines. Lawrence was a young gentleman of about twenty-two years of age and a psychology major in college. He was very loyal and always there for me in my time of need, whether it was helping with finances or just needing to talk. Even though he was much younger than I was, his age never came into play. He was sort of an "old soul." Lawrence stayed in touch with me either by phone, instant messages online, e-mail, or letters. He had a genuine character that I adored. Every time we spoke, our conversations lasted for over an hour, sometimes two. We never seemed to be at a loss for words. I told him that we were approved for the home in Marietta and before I could ask, he stated that he would come to Pennsylvania to move us down to Georgia. He was a good person with a good heart and I appreciated him and his friendship. I always told him how wonderful I thought he was and he would tell me that I was the wonderful one and that I gave him too much credit. Throughout my communication with Lawrence in dealing with mother's health, the mistake I made with Thomas, and Robert's ignorance, Lawrence was always there with enlightening words that eased my soul. It seemed like whatever I perceived to be a "problem," he had an answer for it with some encouraging words and I no longer looked at it as a "problem" anymore. In my year long dealings with Lawrence, he taught me about having patience when it came to certain things in my life, like wanting to get back to Georgia so soon and getting my business back on its feet. He taught me about remaining calm when I would feel overwhelmed by the full plate of my present. Lawrence would often state that old religious saying of "The Lord wouldn't put any more on me than I could bear."

Our relationship was quite different. Lawrence respected me. He knew of the pain I endured from my marriage to Robert and the incident with Thomas. He was never pushy, but extremely understanding of my not wanting to be in a boyfriend/girlfriend- type of relationship. Even though Lawrence and I had known each other for a year, I never told anyone about him. Not even my kids. I kind of kept him under my hat. It just seemed to me that whenever I talked to someone like Janet about a guy, she always had that sound in her voice as if to say, "Here she goes again." Then Rolonda was another story. She always said that no one was good enough for me. They just didn't understand that there were some brotha's out there that actually had morals and respect for women and I happened to be friends with one of them. After being packed up and ready to move, Lawrence called to inform me that he and his cousin Sam were on their way up via Greyhound to move us to Georgia. It took them 18 hours to get to Pennsylvania. I made sure that I was there to greet them at the bus station. It was nice seeing Lawrence again after our many e-mails, phone calls, and letters. We embraced each other for quite a few lasting moments. Seeing him again was like a breath of fresh air. At that moment, I felt complete. Lawrence understood me and it didn't matter how much younger he was than I and it didn't matter that he wasn't quite as established yet as Robert was. All that mattered to me was that he treated me like a queen. I liked him a lot and he was winning my heart. I let him know just how much I appreciated him and all that he had done for me.

After we finished with our long hug, he introduced me to his cousin Sam, whom I thanked for coming along to help. From the bus station, we drove to the rented truck center to pick up the moving truck that was reserved for us through Mother. While I drove the car, Lawrence and Sam followed me in the truck to Mother's home. After we got there, I introduced everyone and we began loading. It took us about two hours to load everything completely onto the truck, but it was a fun two hours with Lawrence and his joking. He always managed to put a smile on my face even when I didn't feel like smiling. As we were completely finished, my grandparents, Aunt Ellen, and Rosa came to say goodbye. Needless to say, everyone started getting teary-eyed. I was going to miss them, but at the same time, I was so excited to finally be getting back home to Georgia. While mother was still outside saying goodbye, the girls piled up into the car, and Sam into the truck, Lawrence and I stole a quiet moment in the empty apartment. He took me by the hand and proceeded to tell me just how much he cared for me and that no matter how long it took for me to become ready for a commitment, that he was willing to wait. He expressed a desire to want to get to know my children better and promised me that he would make me happy in every way. He stated that he knew I wasn't ready, but he wanted me to know exactly how he felt about me. I was very grateful for Lawrence being a part of my life and decided to keep what he said in mind. He was definitely everything I was looking for in a man as far as strong shoulders from a mental aspect, honesty, understanding, and sincerity, but I decided to keep our friendship at the level that it was for a while. Who knew what the future may bring. I loved Lawrence and most certainly appreciated him. Maybe he was my "happily ever after." Only time would tell. He accepted my answer of wanting to take my time, but vowed to continue to be there for me.

I needed to know that, as well as hear it. After all the tears and goodbyes, we headed down the road to Georgia. While following Lawrence and Sam in the moving truck, driving Mother's car, my mind began to reminisce. I experienced a quick flash of all the negative happenings of my past that brought me to the present moment and then suddenly, I felt an overwhelming peace that took over my soul. I took it as a sign that my past was no longer a part of my present or future.

I was on my way to a new beginning and a fresh start on life. I had Mother with me, which made me happy to know that she could begin living comfortably. I had my three little ladies by my side. My business began bringing me clientele from having my commercial shown while in Pennsylvania. I finally received my reimbursement of $200 from Thomas Howard via mail a week and a half before moving. My divorce was finalized with Robert and the girls and I were receiving child support from wage garnishment, which meant on time payments. I was going back home to Georgia to continue the expansion of my company and I had a loyal, special friend that made me feel beautiful every time we spoke. God answered my prayers and finally…I exhaled.

www.ingramcontent.com/pod-product-compliance
Lightning Source LLC
LaVergne TN
LVHW051200080426
835508LV00021B/2723

* 9 7 8 0 9 8 2 6 6 9 0 0 6 *